U0558777

The Macat Library
世界思想宝库钥匙丛书

解析约翰·洛克

《政府论》

AN ANALYSIS OF

JOHN LOCKE'S

TWO TREATISES

OF

GOVERNMENT

Jeremy Kleidosty　　Ian Jackson ◎ 著

曹思宇 ◎ 译

上海外语教育出版社
外教社 SHANGHAI FOREIGN LANGUAGE EDUCATION PRESS

目　录

CONTENTS

引 言

要 点

- 约翰·洛克（John Locke）生于 1632 年，是英国著名哲学家。
- 在《政府论》中，他反对"君权神授"论，认为君主对国家的统治源自人民的授权。
- 洛克的思想在当时实属激进，是经典自由主义政治哲学＊的源头。

约翰·洛克其人

《政府论》的作者约翰·洛克 1632 年 8 月 26 日生于英格兰萨默赛特郡。他的父亲是律师，内战期间＊曾在议会派部队担任军官。英国内战冲突的双方是支持查理一世＊的保皇派＊和要求政府权力归于议会的议会派。＊得益于父亲的地位，约翰·洛克被送至伦敦，就读于声名赫赫的西敏公学。

从西敏公学毕业后，洛克赴牛津大学深造，并于 1656 年获学士学位。他的学习之旅并未就此停歇，于 1658 年和 1674 年又相继取得硕士学位和一个医学学位。离开大学后，洛克做过当时极具影响力的政治家沙夫茨伯里伯爵＊的私人医师。他还以医师的身份赴法国工作过，并在之后为英国政府效力期间积累了一些和国际贸易相关的经验。

英国内战从 1642 年一直持续到 1651 年。这促使很多有识之士思考究竟怎样的政府对这个国家最为有益。政治理论家罗伯特·菲尔莫（Robert Filmer）＊和哲学家托马斯·霍布斯（Thomas Hobbes）＊是其中极具代表性的两位人物。他们得出了相似的结论：只有国王才能确保社会中的每一个人都能遵纪守法。他们坚信，国王的权力是上帝赋予的——即君主的统治权神圣不可侵犯。* 洛克对此并不认同，他于1679年至1689年间撰写了《政府论》来驳斥这种观点。这部作品当时不得不匿名发表，主要也是因为他的理念在那个年代极具争议。

1683年，洛克卷入了旨在刺杀国王查理二世 * 的黑麦公馆案（Rye House Plot）。* 查理二世虽是新教徒，* 却私下同情罗马天主教。事实上，他的兄弟詹姆士 * 就是天主教徒。这次暗杀行动的策划者是一伙坚决反对天主教的新教徒，他们担心查理二世死后，英国会再度被罗马天主教统治。由于国王没有子嗣，他的兄弟詹姆士将继承王位。这些新教徒相信，只要成功刺杀查理二世，他们就可以阻止罗马天主教徒重掌王权。洛克卷入此案，是因为他替一名主谋安排了入住黑麦公馆的相关事宜。然而，暗杀失败了。查理二世严厉惩处参与此案的新教骨干分子，洛克被迫流亡荷兰，直到威廉三世 * 成为英格兰新王为止。这就是现今为人所熟知的1688年光荣革命。*

《政府论》的主要内容

虽然当时世界上绝大多数国家都实行君主制，却鲜有关于该政体合理性的讨论。但在英国，关于王权行使范围的争论愈演愈烈，使得国家权力的分配成为一个极其重要的问题。

1649年，查理一世被送上断头台，而内战也使整个英格兰付出惨重代价。这段记忆犹新的血淋淋的教训为洛克的政治学著作提供了重要的历史语境。洛克动笔撰写《政府论》时，英格兰正处于查理一世之子查理二世的统治之下，关于王权界限的老问题再一次被摆上台面。

部分人士认为，战争证明了国家需要一个强势的君主来维持秩序。以菲尔莫和霍布斯为代表的思想家们坚信，如果没有了君主，这个国家会变得四分五裂。在《政府论》的开篇，洛克就针对王权的由来和菲尔莫展开了辩论。在洛克看来，王权并非受之于天，而是源自其所统治的人民。洛克的论断并未局限于探讨英格兰民众应该选择何种政治制度，而是探寻一种具有"普世性"的结论——一个和"全世界所有人"的权益都休戚相关的政治逻辑判断。

洛克在论述中大量引用圣经、自然科学的相关用语，甚至毫不避讳地引用了和他意见相左的霍布斯的一些表述。在《政府论》中，洛克并没有在历史真实性的考据方面浪费过多精力，而是专注于探讨历史的构建与逻辑思辨发展的过程，以此来阐释他的社会观。

在洛克看来，最初人们的生活处于一种"自然状态"。* 他认为，社会的形成是为了让人们能够裁定何人拥有财产。财产的概念对洛克而言极为重要，因为他相信在自然状态下，万物都没有被赋予价值概念，人也不具有对任何事物的占有权。但洛克对此提出了一个疑问，如果这样的论述是正确的，那么财产的概念究竟从何而来？

他首先提出，曾几何时人们可以随意获取自己想要的任何事物，只要确保之后其他人在需要时仍能得到这样东西即可。当人口尚未膨胀时，这并不是什么问题。但当土地和资源变得稀缺，为他人预留所需资源，实现各取所需的愿景就变得不再现实。洛克认为，一部分人通过辛勤劳作使自己的资源效益最大化。比如，一个农民的劳动和土地结合产生的粮食多于自然环境下土地的产能——

这就是所有权概念的萌芽。

　　财产的问题在于它可能被任何人窃取。因此保护个人财产不被他人窃取的法律变得十分重要。当然，法律需要政治权力来背书，所以人们需要建立某种形式的政府来确保所有人都能遵守新法令。就大部分的人类历史来看，这意味着拥立一位君主来维系社会秩序。

　　洛克为此引入了一个全新的概念，称之为"契约"。虽然人民仍然保有权利，但他们需要让渡自己的部分权利来换取君主对自己（及财产）的保护。君主须确保人民和谐相处——但在洛克看来，这并不意味着国王能凌驾于法律之上。契约的效力是双向的。如果君主触犯法律，那么就应该换其他人来统治。

《政府论》的学术价值

　　洛克的理论描绘了一个与当时社会截然不同的政治图景，这无疑是具有革命性的。他认为，人民应该对由何人来治理国家保有发言权。如果一个政府不能确保人民的利益，那么他支持人民将其推翻。

　　1704 年洛克逝世后，包括苏格兰哲学家大卫·休谟 * 在内的许多重要思想家进一步拓展了他的理论。待到 18 世纪后期，这些理论已成显学。1775 年至 1783 年间，十三个英属殖民州 * 发起的美国独立战争 * 就是以洛克关于人民无需顺从恶政的观点为基础的。以政治理论家托马斯·潘恩 * 和托马斯·杰斐逊 * 为代表的许多革命人士都赞成洛克的理论。独立战争胜利后，他们创立了一种和洛克理念相似的政府形式。在这种新的政府组织中，没有君主，设立选举制度，政府必须保障人民权利。

现如今，这些"自由（主义）"理念*似乎让人觉得习以为常。得益于洛克的贡献，自由主义成了历史上最成功的政治运动之一。这些理念在启蒙时代*萌芽于欧洲，掀起了崇尚理性的思潮。之后在年轻的美利坚生根发芽，证明了一个自由主义的国家并不会像霍布斯们所警告的那样变得四分五裂。那是一个风起云涌的时代。在法兰西，人民经过审判，把之前几乎享有绝对权力的国王送上断头台，建立了一个属于人民的共和国。

　　对生活在自由主义民主国家*的人而言，当下的政治制度得益于洛克观点的启发。比如，具有深远影响力的《美国宪法》*以其构思保障了美国公民的权利。该宪法就是以洛克的哲学为基础起草的。直到今天，它仍然对美国政治起着举足轻重的作用。

　　今天，当人民感到政府权力的扩张是以牺牲人民自由为代价时（如人民的言论自由和隐私权受到威胁），洛克的理论仍然会彰显其价值。虽然许多重要思想家对洛克的观点做出了修正和扩展，他仍被视作经典自由主义之父。如果没有《政府论》，我们现在所生活的世界绝对会是另外一幅景象。

第一部分：学术渊源

1 作者生平与历史背景

要点 ⚷

- 《政府论》是政治哲学领域最伟大的作品之一。在1704年约翰·洛克逝世后很长一段时间内都保持了巨大影响力。

- 洛克生前是社会显要之士，接受的是当时最好的教育。

- 英格兰曾有过在没有君主的情况下治理国家的历史。虽然算不上多么成功，但和君主制统治的情况相比并不逊色。这就引发了一个疑问，到底哪个制度才是最好的？

为什么要读这部著作？

对于约翰·洛克在《政府论》中许多观点的原创性存在大量争论。但一般而言，财产权*演化及其和国家的创建与功能之间关系的论述被认为是他对政治学思想的主要贡献。[1] 不仅如此，他所提出的何种情况下可以合理地推翻统治者的重要观点对18世纪动荡不堪的政治格局产生了直接影响。[2]

尽管《政府论》致力于为当时不少意识形态和政治行为做辩护，但并没有不加甄别地全盘支持或否定任何主流思想。他对殖民主义*的辩护和他否定暴政并呼吁人民起来反抗的观点甚至有些自相矛盾。[3]

然而，即使在洛克去世后，这部作品依然保持着重要影响力。它启发人们建立了美利坚合众国，影响了如激进政治理论家托马斯·潘恩*、哲学家大卫·休谟*和政治哲学家让·雅克·卢梭*在内的重要思想家。因此，这部作品始终都被视作政治哲学最伟

8

大的作品之一。如果不清楚洛克的观点以及这些观点此后在政治实践中的应用，那么就不可能对西方政治思想的演化过程有完整的认知。

> "这个世界上的土地原本足够供养两倍于现在的人口。但随着货币的创造，以及人们心照不宣地为货币赋予统一的价值，产生了扩大财产拥有权的诉求。"
>
> —— 约翰·洛克:《政府论》

作者生平

洛克的父亲是一名英格兰律师，略有余财。他把儿子送进了名校，而洛克也因优异的表现被牛津大学录取。在牛津时，洛克研习政治学、医学和自然科学。[4] 尽管学识出众，自己的出身阶层也和政治圈不乏联系，但真正决定他前途的是他和当时社会权贵们的往来。这其中就包括那位颇具影响力的政治家——沙夫茨伯里伯爵一世。*

要理解洛克的著作，就不能将其意涵和他的社会教育背景割裂开来，也不能无视作品和他的社交圈之间的联系。从 17 世纪中叶开始，宗教冲突和内战使英格兰陷入了严重的动荡。政治阶层中的每一个人都被迫在罗马天主教 * 和新教 * 教义、共和制 * 和君主制 * 等选项之间给出明确答案。

作为一个新教教徒的儿子，在伦敦西敏公学和牛津大学接受教育，这样的背景促使洛克去构建一种关于国家的历史叙事来解释国家的自然与社会起源。[5] 这样的论述削弱了宗教对君主和政府权力合法性的辩护。这种历史叙事也让他为殖民主义做出辩护，对财产权利做出解释。在帝国扩张和资本主义发展的时期*，这些都是人们最为关切的核心议题。

虽然洛克从未试图掩盖自己哲学观点的矛盾之处，也从来没有表明自己从属于任何特定的思想流派，但他和沙夫茨伯里伯爵的关系在实质上对他的政治观乃至世界观产生了影响。因为伯爵的关系，洛克参与了一些重要的政治活动，如卡罗莱纳殖民州（现今美国的北卡与南卡两州所在地）的管理，以及被许多历史学家称为"王位排除危机"（exclusion crises）*的一系列政治事件。这些政治活动旨在阻止笃信罗马天主教的詹姆士二世*继承信奉新教的查理二世*的王位。洛克似乎从心底感到惧怕，担心一个信仰罗马天主教的君主会将这个大多数人信仰新教的国家拖入又一场宗教战争。[6]

正因为如此，恐怕也只有洛克在那个特定的历史语境下能够完成《政府论》这样一部著作。他以前所未有的方式驳斥了王权神圣不可侵犯*（即君权神授）的观点。

创作背景

洛克撰写《政府论》的历史语境曾引发广泛讨论。尽管文本写作的确切时间（一般认为写作时间是 1679 年至 1689 年间）不详，它的历史背景相对而言比较容易确定。

在处决了查理一世*后，英格兰经历了 19 年没有君主的岁月。但在 1660 年，君主制复辟。虽然不是所有人都拥护新王查理二世，但到了他统治的末期，围绕着他的继任人选的疑虑成了政治焦点。查理二世没有合法子嗣，这意味着他的兄弟詹姆士二世将会在他死后成为国王。这对很多人而言是不可接受的，因为詹姆士独断专行，拒绝和议会*合作。更重要的是，他还是一名众所周知的罗马天主教教徒。

1685 年，查理二世去世，詹姆士二世也确实成了国王，但他的统治却持续不到三年。1688 年，詹姆士流亡海外，信奉新教的威廉·奥伦治*和妻子玛丽*取代他，被拥立为新王和女王。这便是后人所熟知的"光荣革命"。*

这些都说明，该著作的发表时间（1689 年）具有重要意义。随着詹姆士二世统治的终结，关于如何治理国家的探讨变得十分紧迫。由于被错误地指控参与了黑麦公馆案，*企图刺杀查理二世，洛克从 1683 年开始一直在荷兰流亡。直到 1688 年光荣革命之后才陪同未来的女王玛丽二世返回英国。

无论洛克撰写《政府论》的确切时间是哪一年，作品在 1689 年发表本身就说明当时英格兰的政治局势仍不明朗。

---

1. 彼得·拉斯莱特："约翰·洛克概论"，《政府论》（第二版），彼得·拉斯莱特 编，剑桥：剑桥大学出版社，1988 年，第 101 页。

2. V. C. 切珀：《剑桥洛克研究指南》，剑桥：剑桥大学出版社，1994 年，第 228 页。

3. 详见约翰·洛克：《政府论》（下篇）第五章"论财产"和第十八章"论暴政"。

4. 拉斯莱特：《政府论》概述，第 17—24 页。

5. 拉斯莱特：《政府论》概述，第 18—22 页，第 40—45 页。

6. 详见大卫·阿米塔吉："约翰·洛克、卡罗莱纳与《政府论》"，载《政治学理论》32，2004 年第 5 期，第 602—627 页；拉斯莱特：《政府论》概述，第 25—44 页。

2 学术背景

要点 🔑━━

- 《政府论》是最早研究探讨自由主义政治哲学*的著作之一。

- 在百家争鸣及崇尚理性的启蒙时代*，人民权利和国家权力等根深蒂固的观念开始受到质疑。

- 洛克开始从自然与社会的角度来思考国家治理的模式，摒弃了王权受之于天的宗教观念。

著作语境

约翰·洛克在《政府论》中表达了自由主义政治哲学思想。其关注的焦点是个人权利。

由于存在着这样一种共识，即不能赋予人民绝对的自由去随心所欲地行事，因此很自然地得出这样一个结论：政府必须保有某种权力来防止无政府状态*（即没有政府或法律的社会）的产生。尽管权利与自由的观念早已深入人心，但在《政府论》出版的 1689年，情况却大不相同。事实上，当时很多人认为君主凌驾于法律之上——当然，和法兰西相比，这种观念在英格兰的影响稍弱一些，毕竟英格兰民众在历史上早已享有一定程度的公民自由（人民只服从那些被认定有益于大众福祉的法律）。

1642 年至 1651 年的英国内战*爆发的导火索就是查理一世*是否需要就提高税收的问题对议会*负责。对君主问责的想法在那个时代显得过于惊世骇俗。最终，直到美国独立战争*（1775 年—1783 年）之后，洛克的理念才被付诸实践。当时，以哲学家大卫·休谟*为代表的思想家们已经对洛克的观点进行了拓展。

得益于洛克的贡献，财产、暴政、政治反抗等议题不再仅仅是抽象的概念。这些问题根植于真实具体的事件，影响着许多民众（尤其是英格兰民众）的生活。与此同时，洛克对于普遍原则的强调有助于说明不同形式的政府和政治信仰之间如何进行互动交流。因此，洛克的观点可以很容易地被运用到那些和他个人生活经验差异巨大的社会语境中。[1]

> "国家统治者不一定非得和国王画等号。它既可以是一个人，也可以由一群人组成。"
>
> —— 托马斯·霍布斯:《利维坦》

学科概览

约翰·洛克撰写《政府论》的语境充斥着政治革命*与争议。洛克也自然不是唯一一个探索这些问题的思想家。罗伯特·菲尔莫*和托马斯·霍布斯*是当时的两位重要人物。他们也在面对同样的难题，却最终得出了截然不同的答案。

菲尔莫的著作《父权制》在1680年他去世后出版，其政治语境和洛克的作品是一致的。对于议会和查理一世之间的冲突最终导致内战的时代背景，《父权制》引用圣经的内容来为君主统治进行辩护。菲尔莫以家庭为例，认为应由父亲掌握支配的权力，死后这份权力应由长子继承。[2]尽管菲尔莫不是唯一一个赞同君主权力神圣不可侵犯的哲学家（即认为君主受命于天，因此具有可以独断专行的权利），但洛克却将批判的矛头单独对准了他。《政府论》上篇的内容事实上就是针对菲尔莫的观点所做的正面驳斥。

总体而言，霍布斯和菲尔莫并非同道中人。前者于 1651 年出版的重要著作《利维坦》写于英国内战的动荡岁月。在这本书中，霍布斯引入了社会契约*的概念，认为政府被组建是因为一个社会群体为了保障成员的生活和基本权利而同意接受一个统治者（或统治阶级）的管理。这一观点暗示了，政府如果不能履行其应尽的职责，那么统治的合法性就不复存在。

这一观点的重要性不容低估。"社会契约"可以被视作一切现代西方政治哲学的根基。和菲尔莫一样，霍布斯也赞成保全君主权力，但后者得出这样的结论是出于实用主义而非神学*层面的考量。在目睹了内战引发的混乱后，霍布斯相信是君主的存在维持了社会稳定，而民众的反叛则造成了动荡失序。

洛克《政府论》下篇的标题表明这部作品旨在理解"政府的真正起源、范围和目的"。洛克的核心观点关注的是国家的起源，是否需要限制君主*的权力、是否需要将权威等同于法律，以及保障政治和财产权利*的重要性。[3]

这些并没有和霍布斯的论断产生直接冲突，因为霍布斯也认同服务民众是权力合法性的基础。同时他也认为只要法律没有明令禁止，人民的行为就不应该受到限制。

但在实践层面，两人的观点几乎完全不同。霍布斯认为自然状态*充满着暴力，人在那种状态下的生活是"孤独、贫穷、肮脏、残暴和难以持久的"。[4]霍布斯作品中的"利维坦"指的是保障人民不互相（且不自我）侵害的君主（或主权国家）。在他看来，人是通过让渡自然权利来换取君主（或主权国家）对自己的保护。

学术渊源

在评价约翰·洛克的《政府论》时，几乎无法回避他的交际圈对他产生的影响。

洛克的教育、宗教和家庭背景促使他从自然和社会的维度去构建一种国家理论。[5] 他的观点对那些试图从宗教层面为君主或议会权力做辩护的人们发起了挑战。洛克和牛津大学的渊源，和沙夫茨伯里伯爵 * 以及约翰·索莫斯 * 等人的友谊都让他有机会去表达和倾听那些激进的观点。

洛克生于动荡变化的年代。古希腊哲学家柏拉图 * 的思想统治欧洲已经两千多年。但一部分人（如洛克同时代的哲学家勒内·笛卡尔 *）开始挑战并试图修正那些经典学说。就这一点而言，洛克的理论受到历史事件和时代精神的双重启发，可视作霍布斯观点的进一步演化。

启蒙运动的理性精神重视新观点，启发人们反思那些根深蒂固的行为方式。洛克固然倡导建立一个由权力受限的君主统治的现代型政府，且这正是他的一些政要朋友所渴望的，但洛克的观点所产生的影响远远超出了 17 世纪的英格兰政坛。

1. 详见理查德·艾什克拉夫特："洛克政治哲学"，V. C. 切珀 编，《剑桥洛克研究指南》，剑桥：剑桥大学出版社，1994 年，第 226—228 页。
2. 详见罗伯特·菲尔莫：《父权制》，约翰·索默维尔 编，伦敦：剑桥大学出版社，1991 年。
3. 切珀：《剑桥洛克研究指南》，第 228—230 页。
4. 托马斯·霍布斯：《利维坦》，韦尔：华兹华斯图书，2014 年，第 97 页。
5. 彼得·拉斯莱特："约翰·洛克概论"，《政府论》（第二版），彼得·拉斯莱特 编，剑桥：剑桥大学出版社，1988 年，第 18—22，第 40—45 页。

3 主导命题

要点 🔑

- 在《政府论》的写作期间，思想家们开始探讨应该如何治理社会。
- 正如许多政治理论家通过不同方式所论证的那样，君权神授是当时的主流观点。
- 洛克延续并发展了霍布斯*的观点，对社会与统治者之间达成契约的条件做出定义。

核心问题

约翰·洛克的《政府论》具备明确的写作目标。可以说作品下篇的副标题对这一目标做出了清楚的说明。洛克希望探讨"政府的真正起源、范围和目的"，并通过理解政治权力的本质来得到答案。[1]

政治权力的源头与终点，以及权力的目的是这部作品以及那个时代所面对的核心问题。这也可以说是所有政治思想都涉及的根本问题之一。成为那个时代的核心问题这件事本身有助于我们理解洛克起初为何要提出这个问题。

这些议题的分歧导致的公民与社会冲突贯穿了洛克的一生。因此，从实践角度来看，不同的答案意味着不同的社会格局：稳定与平和，抑或是不确定性和战争。从更加宏观的角度而言，洛克明白这些问题并非17世纪的英格兰所独有。因此，他没有将写作对象单纯地设定为自己的国家，而是选择运用哲学论证，使他的作品具有"普世性"价值。

> "仰仗着这份信任，他们滥用人民赋予的权力而未履行相应职责。最终人民会收回这份权力。"
>
> —— 约翰·洛克:《政府论》

参与者

《政府论》写作期间的政治氛围所引发的讨论远远超出了学术和政治的范畴。大多数观点都可以被分为截然对立的两种立场，如是支持罗马天主教*还是新教*，拥护王权还是议会权力。[2]

如前文所述，和洛克观点相对立的两则最有影响力的论点都认为这个国家应该由一位君主来统治——尽管两者论据不尽相同。

罗伯特·菲尔莫*的论证在本质上是以圣经经典为依据的。他的思维脉络如果脱离圣经的宗教语境就无法成立。菲尔莫认为，上帝赋予人类始祖亚当管理子孙后代的绝对权力。政治权力通过父亲传递给儿子，这样的系统称之为父权制。*尽管无法追溯一条完整不间断的权力继承脉络，但在菲尔莫看来，权力的传承神圣不可侵犯，且一直延续至今。只有君主可以制定法律，这也意味着君主凌驾于一切法律之上。

和菲尔莫相比，霍布斯*的观点更加贴近现实语境。在霍布斯看来，神灵之说不是探讨政府架构的关键。他更关心的是一个优良的政府需要具备哪些实际条件。霍布斯认为，"自然"不是一个适宜生活的空间状态。尽管霍布斯从荷兰哲学家雨果·格罗修斯*那里借用了这一概念，但他还是通过和自然状态的对比来发展自己的社会契约理论。*

君主的权力不是受之于天，为了换取保护而自愿放弃自由的社会赋予了国王权力。因此霍布斯设想的统治者必须是一个拥有绝对权力的人，他控制着社会的方方面面，从而避免国家陷入弱肉强食的无政府状态。*

洛克拒绝接受这种关于人性的悲观主义观点。他相信人能够创造出宽容、繁荣、保障个人自由的社会。[3]

当代论战

17 世纪的政治思想发展缓慢。洛克可以说是延续并发展了霍布斯开启的思想变革进程（但如前文所述，其实霍布斯从格罗修斯的观点中得到了不少启发）。

《政府论》上篇直接驳斥了菲尔莫的观点，而对于霍布斯的回应则显得较为隐晦。洛克对菲尔莫的态度是完全否定。而对于霍布斯，洛克修正了社会契约理论，以至于最终得出了一个不同的结论。然而，洛克并不是闭门造车得出这些观点的。还有几位思想家也在思考同样的问题，甚至还得出了相似的结论。洛克的好友、政治作家詹姆斯·提雷尔*写了《父权制不等于君主制》。就反驳罗伯特·菲尔莫*的君主专制论*而言，这部作品一开始具有更大的影响力。共和派*人士阿尔戈农·西德尼*的作品《论政府》也将矛头对准菲尔莫，言辞更加激烈。[4]

尽管他的作品从其他思想家的观点中汲取了很多养分，洛克将财产、社会进化以及政治义务等理论结合在一起，创造出一套严密的政治权利学说。这套学说以"普世"原则为基础，为革命的合法性提供了辩护。*比如，霍布斯认为自然状态*的特征是不稳定与财产得不到保障。而洛克拓展了这一表述，认为财产保护实际上构成了人民与政府之间达成社会契约的基础。

　　洛克的影响力绝不局限于 17 世纪。他的观点早已成为西方政治学不可分割的组成部分。受到他影响的思想家包括让·雅克·卢梭*和托马斯·潘恩。*他们提倡所有公民在政治上都是绝对平等的，反对君主制，支持公民遵守法律和自由选举的结果。这让人不得不赞叹，洛克的思想至今仍然保持着影响力。5

1. 约翰·洛克：《政府论》（第二版），彼得·拉斯莱特 编，剑桥：剑桥大学出版社，1988 年，第 267—268 页。

2. 关于写作背景的探讨，详见彼得·拉斯莱特："约翰·洛克概论"，《政府论》，第 45—66 页。

3. 洛克将殖民主义视作构建理想政府的方式，详见芭芭拉·阿内尔：《约翰·洛克和美洲：为英国殖民主义辩护》，牛津：牛津大学出版社，1996 年。

4. 阿尔戈农·西德尼：《论政府》，伦敦：1698 年。登录日期 2015 年 4 月 7 日，http://www.constitution.org/as/dcg_000.htm。

5. 详见马汀·P.汤普森："洛克《政府论》的接受 1690—1750 年"，载《政治学研究》24，1976 年第 2 期，第 184—191 页；另详见埃利斯·桑多斯：《以法为本的政府：政治理论、宗教和美国的建立》（第一卷），哥伦比亚：密苏里大学出版社，2001 年。

4 作者贡献

要点 🔑

- 洛克拒绝接受君权神授、公民必须绝对服从君主的观点。

- 洛克的观点基本建立在社会契约论之上,即社会团体同意接受统治以换取被保护的权利。如果无法保障这一权利,那么政府就失去了其合法性。

- 洛克的作品吸收已有的观点,但在此基础上发展并产生了新的结论和思想。

作者目标

在《政府论》中,约翰·洛克提出了一系列核心观点,并通过全新的方式进行论述。尽管他显然参考了自己在政治实践中积累的经验,但也避免去明确指涉英格兰的历史或法律——这对当时的政治写作是很不寻常的。[1]考虑到赞助人兼好友沙夫茨伯里伯爵一世等人 * 的政治活动和思想(试图干涉英国王位继承),以及洛克对霍布斯 * 思想的吸收修正,显然洛克的写作是对当时学界和政治圈的回应。

他得出结论前首先探讨了自己反对君权神授的观点。这种思考方式和他的医师背景关系紧密。对问题进行诊断,继而提出改进或修正的方法——就好比是医师对症下药。法国政治理论家让·博丹 * 认为保障财产权 * 是自然法 * 的一部分,因此对统治者权力[2]起到了实质性的限制作用。尽管借鉴了博丹等人的观点,洛克思想的独特之处在于,他的结论不仅在理论上具有"普世性"价值,同时也可运用于具体的政治实践。如果这部著作被看成是对正统思想的挑战的话，那么它也确实将其中蕴含的激进观点表现得淋漓尽致。

虽然洛克经常被归入自由主义政治*的传统范畴（强调个人权利、政府职责和限制政府权力），但他的观点同时也具备高度的社群主义意识。在 17 世纪，如此强调个人权利并不常见。两千多年前的柏拉图*就批判过民主*的观点。而当时大多数（如果不是全部的话）的哲学家对经典学说的尊崇甚至可以说是导致了政治学思想的拘泥不化。即使在洛克逝世后，这一现象仍长期存在。

> "只要社会仍然存续，个体在成为社会一份子时所让渡的权力就决不能重新归还个体，而是由社群永远保有完整的权力。若非如此，共同体或共和就都不复存在了。"
>
> —— 约翰·洛克:《政府论》

研究方法

洛克在作品中的遣词用句反映了他参与当时的政治辩论时所要表达的精神。例如，他使用了"公共利益"（common-wealth）一词。这不仅仅是国家（state）的替代语，而是指涉了一个关怀全体公民福祉的国家形态。洛克还说，如果这个共同体的权利福祉被忽视甚至践踏，那么人民就有权用一个新政府去取代旧政府。如果觉得"对大众是有益"的话，他们甚至有权创造全新的政治权力架构。[3]假如说洛克所倡导的民主和今天所理解的民主不尽相同，那么他也确实是在提倡一种以个人主义为基础的民主，鼓励公民和政治阶级之间达成社会契约关系，强调对公共利益的关注。这使得这部作品始终在自由主义政治思想传统中保有一席之地。

同样的，洛克认为国家的起源是达成保障财产的契约，继而进化为由法律取代君主成为国家最高主权代表的系统。这些观点极具开创性。对洛克撰写《政府论》时的英格兰而言，1649 年处死查理一世，*1660 年查理二世复辟，*1688 年罢黜詹姆士二世 * 这些事件仍然令人记忆犹新，桩桩件件都记录了政治派别中一方对另一方的胜利。洛克的论述为废黜两位君主做出辩护，这可以从两个角度来解读。一方面，他真诚地号召人们参与革命；另一方面也认为只有在确认暴政出现的情况下才能废黜某位君主。[4] 换言之，洛克的论述也解释了 17 世纪的英格兰为何会发生一连串严重的社会动荡。

　　有必要指出的是，尽管洛克并未直接提及上述历史事件，但所有读者都应该能理解字里行间所影射的内容。洛克最独特、最深远的贡献就是他不仅为历史事件爆发的原因做出合理辩护，同时倡导在未来构建一种新的政府形式——稳固、有限制任期、遵从人民的意志。

时代贡献

　　在《政府论》下篇第五章中，洛克这样写道："这个世界上的土地原本足够供养两倍于现在的人口。但随着货币的创造，以及人们心照不宣地为货币赋予统一的价值，产生了扩大财产拥有权的诉求。"[5] 他认为货币的发明让人获得多于其实际能够使用的财产，因此引起了原本不会发生的资源短缺。这是洛克关于"自然状态"*思想实验的一部分，即要求人们展开想象，思考社会及相关政治机构出现之前人类的生活是怎样的。

　　《政府论》下篇从霍布斯那里借鉴的社会契约理论占了很大比重。但两人在一个议题上分歧明显。在霍布斯看来，自然状态意味着暴力横行、无法无天、弱肉强食。而洛克却认为，自然状态是受法律支配、信奉理性的。因此，他的贡献就是在既有观点基础上进行拓展，发展出全新的思想和结论。有一些概念（如"人性本善"等）在霍布斯的论述中是看不到的。

这很可能导致读者得出这样一个结论：就社会契约概念而言，洛克的作品和霍布斯有着不可分割的联系。但必须注意两点。首先，洛克的作品上篇是对前人思想的颠覆而非延续。其次，洛克和霍布斯的思考过程类似，但结论完全不同。通过对社会契约概念的重新阐释，洛克最终将读者引向了其所描绘的自由主义国家政体。

1. 关于洛克的一生，详见 J. R. 弥尔顿："洛克生平与时代"，《剑桥洛克研究指南》，V. C. 切珀 编，剑桥：剑桥大学出版社，1994 年，第 5—25 页。

2. 关于洛克的思想渊源，详见马汀·P. 汤普森："洛克《政府论》的接受 1690—1705 年"，载《政治学研究》24，1976 年第 2 期，第 184—185 页。

3. 约翰·洛克：《政府论》（第二版），彼得·拉斯莱特 编，剑桥：剑桥大学出版社，1988 年，第 428 页。

4. 有观点认为洛克想要刻意煽动叛乱，详见理查德·艾什克拉夫特："洛克政治哲学"，《剑桥洛克研究指南》，V. C. 切珀 编，剑桥：剑桥大学出版社，1994 年，第 226—251 页。也有观点认为，洛克的写作动机不明，详见约翰·邓恩：《约翰·洛克政治思想：〈政府论〉的论辩史》，剑桥：剑桥大学出版社，1982 年。

5. 彼得·拉斯莱特："洛克概论"，《政府论》，第 293 页。

第二部分：学术思想

5 思想主脉

要点 🔑

- 洛克认为，虽然公民为了在社会中生存放弃了部分权利，但是其所放弃的权利并非无止境的。

- 洛克对政治权力的起源提出了自己的理论假设，并试图证明其合理性。

- 洛克惯用旧式遣词用句，有时不易理解。但他的论证逻辑能帮助现代读者理解作品的意涵。

核心主题

约翰·洛克在《政府论》中探讨的核心主题是政治权力的起源、政治权力在构建国家机器时的作用、国家权力的界限，以及在何种情况下权力可以被推翻或取代。这些主题还包含了其他一些重要议题，如财产权、*奴隶制、*父权，以及政治分权。

洛克所探讨的主题可以被分为两个部分。

在著作的上篇中，他主要针对的是政治思想家罗伯特·菲尔莫*关于君主绝对权力的论述。菲尔莫将王权和圣经中关于亚当作为所有人类始祖的描述联系在一起。尼科洛·马基雅维利*在《君主论》（*The Prince*）一书中对君主掌权的不同方式进行了罗列分析。[1]而洛克也采用了和后者类似的策略，对菲尔莫有关亚当权力及为英格兰君主制辩护的种种论断做了有力驳斥。

《政府论》下篇所探讨的主题大致相同，但却采纳了"演化发展"的逻辑推演，追溯了自原始社会开始形成的政治权力以及私有财产与货币的发展过程。这一方法让读者能充分理解洛克对于人性、社会、国家，以及构建国家的最终目的的假设。在定义和解释了这些假设之后，他又进一步说明为何国家机器有必要将立法权和执法权分立，国家的统治如何变得腐败，以及社会该如何对权力滥用进行修正。

> "（自然状态下）没有艺术；没有文字；没有社会；最糟糕的是永远处于暴力死亡的恐惧和危险的境地；人类生活在孤单、贫穷、肮脏、残暴、难以持久。"
>
> —— 托马斯·霍布斯:《利维坦》

观点探究

由于这些主题聚焦权力的问题，可以认为这部著作的核心议题之一就是对人权进行定义。洛克并没有鼓吹建立一个完全自由的社会，而是设想在政府和人民之间达成某种契约。

尽管《政府论》上篇有助于下篇的论述，但总体而言两篇的论证是相对独立的。

17 世纪的英格兰社会宗教氛围浓郁，洛克的读者们不得不面对一个受命于天的君主的存在：如果君主的权力是上帝赋予的，那么任何对君权的限制都意味着违逆上帝的意志。这种信仰被称作"绝对主义"（absolutism）。*

通过驳斥菲尔莫的学说（统治者是继承圣经中人类始祖亚当的权力），洛克对绝对主义进行了批判。洛克不认为上帝赋予亚当任何凌驾于子孙后代的权力，并表示在实践层面不可能厘清历史上权力的传承脉络。

假如是在宗教式微的年代，这样的论述也许会显得多此一举。但对洛克的同代人而言，这种观点让他们解放了思想，可以去思考赋予政府权力所需的特定条件。这一论述也让人们得以探讨权力合法性的界限，尤其是思考是否可以更换统治者或改变国家政治架构。

在否定了绝对主义之后，洛克又提出了一种假说，即社会是如何发展成为政治国家的。

1688年光荣革命*中，信奉天主教的詹姆士二世*被信仰新教的威廉三世*和妻子玛丽二世*取代。对洛克的论述主题而言，这一历史背景极其重要，却又往往被刻意忽略。如果认定詹姆士二世滥用了自己的权力，那么或许会觉得洛克是在为废黜他进行辩护。但同时也可以认为威廉和玛丽遵守议会制定的法律，*因而符合洛克认定的理想政治模式。[2]

但是，《政府论》和特定历史事件的关联不应该妨碍读者去认识作品主题所蕴含的"普世"意义。政府必须保障财产权以及人民赋予政府权力等观点引出了一个重要的、符合逻辑的结论：人民赋予权力，亦可收回权力。

如果权力被滥用便可更换统治者。这始终是这部作品最具影响力的观点之一。

语言与表述

尽管对现代读者而言，洛克的文笔显得陈旧晦涩，但他在进行论证时，逻辑严谨清晰。必须指出的是，《政府论》上篇相对而言更难理解。该部分对菲尔莫论点的引述以及关于圣经经典的分析都要求读者对相关文本的内容具备一定程度的了解。

然而，洛克的分析方式是层层推演的，各篇幅之间互相支持印证，从而有助于读者理解 17 世纪英语的表达方式。洛克的观点论述严密且包罗万象，启发了许许多多政治家、政法学者与政治理论家。

洛克以财产权为基础的政治权力分析的影响力尤为深远。通过创造"公共利益"（common-wealth）*等全新概念，他提倡建立一个人人享有物质繁荣权利的社会。这一观点极具政治影响力，超出了纯粹的激进言论的范畴，引发了大量的辩论。其论点与精神也在美国《独立宣言》*等政治文本中被引用。在《独立宣言》中，北美殖民地人民 * 抵抗英国统治的理论依据很大程度上来自洛克对于违反财产权和个人隐私的批判。美国及其宪法理念在国际事务中长久以来占据统治地位。这就使得洛克学说的影响力变得尤为深远。[3]因此，洛克被视作自由主义之父——尽管他本人从未在《政府论》中使用过"自由主义"一词。

洛克的学说完整且富有逻辑性，但也必然存在不够成熟的地方。他所描绘的是一种理想化的政府形式，却无意将这种设想应用到改造当时政府架构的实践中去。直到 1776 年《独立宣言》发表以及年轻的美利坚取得独立战争的胜利，洛克的这些观点才真正被运用于政治实践。

1. 尼科洛·马基雅维利：《君主论》，乔治·鲍尔 译，伦敦：企鹅出版社，1987 年。
2. 洛克撰写《政府论》的直接动机和光荣革命的关系，详见鲁瓦·G. 施瓦雷："洛克、洛克思想和光荣革命",载《思想史期刊》51, 1990 年第 4 期，第 531—548 页。

3. 关于美国法律和洛克的更多讨论，包括洛克思想在国际语境中的变化发展，详见埃利斯·桑多斯：《以法为本的政府：政治理论、宗教和美国的建立》（第一卷），哥伦比亚：密苏里大学，2001 年。

6 思想支脉

要点 🔑

- 洛克对殖民主义*和奴隶制*等主题的强调。

- 《政府论》从财产的角度谈及美洲殖民地。*洛克认为相比美洲原住民，欧洲人能够更好地开发利用那里的土地。

- 洛克对权力在宗教层面的合法性以及死后将财产和头衔传给长子进行探讨。洛克的这些观点对于我们今天的思考仍有参考价值。

其他观点

殖民主义和奴隶制是《政府论》中涉及的最重要的次要主题，有必要和洛克的宏观论断联系在一起加以思考。

关于奴隶制的讨论是为了展现君权神授理论*以及绝对（专制）主义*所带来的危险后果。洛克认为："一个人既然没有创造自己生命的能力，就不能用契约或通过同意把自己交由任何人奴役，或置身于别人的绝对的、任意的权力之下，任其剥夺自己的生命。"[1]

这样一来，洛克就为论述自然权利*打下了基础，也为最终废除奴隶制提供了理论依据。和洛克的许多其他观点一样，他所描绘的是一个理想国家的面貌。多年之后，废奴才真正成为现实。

洛克相信财产保障的诉求是政治社会形成的原动力，其涉及美洲和原住民的论述也和这一论述有着紧密联系。他通过这个例子来证明自己关于社会发展的假设性推论是具有现实意义的。但同时，他又利用这个例子来为英格兰殖民的合法性进行辩护，认为相比美洲原住民，英格兰人对土地的利用开发更有效，因而能为大众带来更多的利益。[2]和大量引用圣经经典来驳斥父权制*的方式不同，洛克在探讨奴隶制问题时的论证生动易懂。他首先表示人的劳动和（土地）财产的结合产生了财产权，紧接着他认为殖民扩张使得之前未充分利用的土地获得了更多劳动力而增值，因此殖民行为具有合法性。[3]

> "谁都不能把多于自己所有的权力给予他人；凡是不能剥夺自己生命的人，就不能把支配自己生命的权力给予别人。"
>
> —— 约翰·洛克：《政府论》

观点探究

除了论证政治权力应该受到约束并且以公众利益为基础，洛克涉及的次级主题则致力于探讨这样一个问题：在能够证明对大众有益的前提下，一国是否有权干涉其他国家的内部事务。

在洛克看来，财产权利是不可触及的底线，因此所有权的问题十分紧迫。虽然这些观点涉及这部作品的核心主题，但却在美洲殖民地的议题上显得尤为关键。根据洛克的观点，财产权神圣不可侵犯。因此要为剥夺土著人的土地进行辩护，非得花一番工夫不可。

乍一看，殖民统治和自由主义*政治思想显得格格不入。对这一问题感兴趣的学生和学者也常常会通过洛克对殖民主义的辩护和他对美洲的描述来思考这一悖论。[4]

尽管这部作品探讨的是个人的政治与财产权利，但对于那些思考两性在社会中的权力关系基础以及是否可以干涉他国事务的人而言，洛克的观点同样具有重要价值。

奴隶制是另一个重要主题。洛克在《政府论》上篇中全面而又系统地驳斥了父权制，认为《圣经》可以为个人权利以及政治平等提供依据。[5] 这些观点很自然地被运用到涉及奴隶制的讨论中。关于这个议题，洛克认为有必要强调任何单一个体的权力都需要受到限制。

当前研究的不足

总体而言，尽管《政府论》是洛克最常被引用的作品，也一般被认为是自由主义和关于"普世"人权*的现代政治思想领域的奠基之作。[6] 但绝大多数研究都集中在作品下篇的部分内容里。

关于上篇的内容，学界兴趣寥寥，也很少有其他重要政治著作引用。而原本对洛克反对父权制*以及无条件的政治顺从的那点兴趣，也随着时间的推移逐渐减弱。

鉴于自由主义民主在世界政治中的突出地位，从现代的视角来看，要理解洛克从理性层面对君权神授*观点的否定，以及他关于滥用公民赋予的权力的可能性这一论断变得更加困难。然而，《政府论》上篇中透露的观点并没有因为时间的推移而失去价值。这些思想对于理解当今的威权统治*的影响有着重要的指导意义。

包括历史学家赫伯特·罗恩（Herbert Rowen）*在内的一些思想家认为，著作上篇之所以被学界忽视，部分原因是对该文本的双重属性认识不足。[7] 这部著作并不仅仅针对罗伯特·菲尔莫*的君权神授理论作了批判。同时洛克也认为，权力必须实行嫡长子继承制。*（财产和头衔必须由长子或嫡子继承）这一观点从本质上来说是错误的。[8] 实际上，作品上篇对政治思想中的弊病做出诊断，而下篇则根据诊断开出药方。

事实上，作品上篇大量引用分析圣经的内容遭到忽视，反映出长久以来学界并没有严肃思考宗教对政治的影响。然而，西方的政治理论家们已经开始重新审视政治思想形成过程中宗教发挥的作用。同样地，政治学家芭芭拉·阿内尔（Barbara Arneil）*等学者认为，洛克关于美洲以及土著群体的部分论述要么遭到忽视，要么被误读。这些内容（主要见于作品第五章）为重新阐释该作品对殖民统治以及资本主义*扩张所做的辩护提供了翔实的材料。9

大卫·黑尔德（David Held）*致力于在倡导"普世"人权以及尊重地方习俗以及道德价值的诉求上达到平衡。包括他在内的很多人权理论家们在评价洛克作品时也采用了相同的策略。相比洛克所处的时代，如今的政治经济全球化*浪潮使得解决两者之间的冲突变得更为紧迫。原因很简单，大多数国家现在都需要遵守各式各样的国际法。这些法令要求，国家对内必须对某些人权给予尊重，而当这些权利得不到保障时，就可能产生干预他国内政的情况。10

---

1. 约翰·洛克：《政府论》（第二版），彼得·拉斯莱特 编，剑桥：剑桥大学出版社，1988 年，第 284 页。

2. 芭芭拉·阿内尔：《约翰·洛克和美洲：为英国殖民主义辩护》，牛津：牛津大学出版社，1996 年，第 1—2 页。

3. 约翰·洛克：《政府论》，第 290—302 页。亦可参考阿内尔：《约翰·洛克和美洲》。

4. 芭芭拉·阿内尔："印第安人的鹿肉：洛克的财产理论和美洲的英格兰殖民"，

载《政治学研究》44，1996 年第 1 期，第 60—74 页。

5. 洛克：《政府论》，171—195 页。

6. 例如，迈克尔·E. 古德哈特："人权问题辩论的起源和普世性：文化本质主义和全球化挑战"，载《人权季刊》25，2003 年第 4 期，935—964 页。

7. 详见赫伯特·H. 罗恩："再议洛克《政府论》"，载《思想史期刊》17，1956 年第 1 期，130—132 页。

8. 同上，130—132 页。

9. 详见阿内尔：《约翰·洛克和美洲》。

10. 详见古德哈特："人权问题辩论的起源和普世性"。

7 历史成就

要点 ⚷—

- 后世认为洛克的观点十分重要。《独立宣言》主要起草人托马斯·杰斐逊＊将他称之为最重要的三位现代思想家之一。
- 美国独立战争＊为洛克关于合格政府的观点提供了有力论证。
- 部分宗教思想家对这部作品进行了批判，认为过度强调个人权利，却忽视了个体对于他人应尽的义务。

观点评析

尽管洛克的《政府论》主要反映了 17 世纪后期英格兰的政治哲学思潮，但相比作品发表的时代，一般认为它对当代的政治论辩更加重要。部分原因在于，18 世纪的思想家们对这部著作评价颇高。如哲学家大卫·休谟＊就表示，《政府论》准确把握了当时众多政治观点的本质。而托马斯·杰斐逊则更是将洛克称为三位最重要的现代思想家之一。[1]

很可能连洛克自己都未能完全认识到自己的论述所蕴含的全部意义。1688 年光荣革命＊后威廉·奥伦治登上英格兰王位成为威廉三世＊，洛克的作品有助于解释当时紧张的政治气氛。事实上，作品于 1689 年出版时，英格兰议会＊已经成功地限制了王权。所以从某种角度来说，洛克所描绘的可算是一种业已存在的政治制度。虽然《政府论》的起草时间早于君主立宪＊的出现，但它实际出版时该制度已经成为了政治现实。从这方面看，很明显洛克是在为新的政治制度做辩护。

然而，这一全新的政治制度并不能真实地反映人民的意志。实际上，就如何管理国家而言，绝大多数民众并没有发言权。很多权力仍旧为君主所掌控，而"真正"的民主*多年之后才会在英格兰出现。所以必须要认识到，尽管民主原则可视作洛克社会契约论的逻辑终点，但他并非在宣扬建立一个民主社会。*洛克之后的思想家们（如让·雅克·卢梭*）才开始强调实行更大范围的公民参政。

> "我们认为这些真理是不言而喻的：人人生而平等，造物者赋予他们若干不可剥夺的权利，其中包括生命权、自由权和追求幸福的权利。"
>
> ——《美国独立宣言》

历史成就

启蒙运动*的主要知识分子，如休谟、托马斯·杰斐逊和政治哲学家孟德斯鸠（Charles Montesquieu）*都在不同情况下引述过洛克的《政府论》。洛克尝试解释知识的分类，并且从非宗教视角论述自然法。*休谟对此甚是赞同。同时他也很欣赏洛克的作品反映了那些主张君主须对议会负责的英格兰政治家们的思想全貌。[2]实际上，自18世纪70年代美国独立战争*反抗不列颠统治以来，洛克的作品就被当做具有权威性的宣言，论述了政府权力源于人民，同时也必须服务于人民的政治原则。随着第二次世界大战*后自由主义*在国际法中占据统治地位，洛克关于国家合法性、国际干预以及政治叛乱在何种情况下是合理的观点变得越来越重要。

在洛克的时代，很难预见到众多国家需要履行国际法（如遵守联合国*原则宗旨*的义务）。当某一国家人民的权利和生命（或生活方式）遭到严重威胁时，签署公约的国家需要对其进行干涉。

尽管《政府论》下篇为殖民主义*和欧洲统治做了辩护，[3]它的观点（尤其在第五、十九章中）可以用来论证：当公民的共同利益受到严重威胁时，其他国家可以对该主权国*的内部事务进行干涉。作品上篇中否定父权*是政治权力的基础。这一观点后来成为历代女权主义者*的重要理论来源。

在美国，洛克被视作政治理论的奠基人之一。在政治论辩中，每每涉及政府是否权力过大或者出现权力滥用的问题，洛克的观点时常会被引用。这些问题包括反对新税收（右派人士认为这是对私人财产的窃取）以及倡导更好地保障言论自由和个人隐私。*

历史局限性

在不同的政治和时空语境中，洛克的《政府论》可以得到不同的阐释。现如今"君权神授"或"王命不可违"的说法是真是假早已不是热门的政治议题。但洛克认为政府必须对人民负责，人民有权推翻暴政。这些观点渗透进了大众意识之中，在自由主义国家中早已被当做政治真理。

非西方和非信仰基督教的读者在理解《政府论》上篇时可能会觉得困难。但剩余的篇幅内容启发人们在不同的政治语境中参与抗争运动，追求个人自由和政治责任，如美国的民权运动*以及20世纪40年代以来风起云涌的去殖民化*浪潮。过去的读者会认为作品下篇的内容是在为殖民统治有利于美洲原住民的观点做辩护。而现如今这些曾经受到殖民压迫的原住民却引用洛克关于政治正义的观点，要求保障财产权和尊重共同体利益。[4]

对洛克作为自由主义思想奠基人的评价和该书自发表之日起得

到的评价是一致的。该书一直被视作对必须保障个人政治权利的有力论证，同时却又在政治镇压和自然法是否具有"普世性"*等问题上显得自相矛盾。在一些持非西方文化的社群主义*视角者（即认为集体利益先于个人利益）来看，洛克的作品过度强调了个人权利却轻视应承担的政治义务。事实上，这样的批评也存在于西方文化语境中。尤其在那些笃信宗教的思想家们看来，这种个人主义忽视了个体对他人应尽的责任。[5]

尽管存在这些局限性，《政府论》仍可以被视作当代自由主义政治思想关于国家权力的核心论述。国家权力源于人民，人民也有权对权力滥用等行为拨乱反正。[6]洛克的作品对此做出了有力的论证。

1. 详见大卫·休谟：《人类理解研究》（第三卷），牛津：牛津大学出版社，2000年，xxxi，第149页。亦可参考彼得·拉斯莱特："约翰·洛克概论"，《政府论》（第二版），剑桥：剑桥大学出版社，1988年，第14—15页。
2. 马汀·P. 汤普森："洛克《政府论》的接受1690—1705年"，载《政治学研究》24，1976年第2期，第184页。
3. 详见芭芭拉·阿内尔："印第安人的鹿肉：洛克的财产理论和美洲的英格兰殖民"，载《政治学研究》44，1996年第1期，第60—74页。
4. 详见芭芭拉·阿内尔："印第安人的鹿肉：洛克的财产理论和美洲的英格兰殖民"，载《政治学研究》44，1996年第1期，第60—74页。
5. 拉斯莱特："《政府论》概述"，第121—122页。
6. 详见拉斯莱特："《政府论》概述"，第122页。亦可参考埃利斯·桑多斯：《以法为本的政府：政治理论、宗教和美国的建立》（第一卷），哥伦比亚：密苏里大学出版社，2001年。

8 著作地位

要点 ⌐━━

- 约翰·洛克晚年撰写的《政府论》是他最后一部政治哲学著作。
- 洛克对很多不同的议题进行过论述，但所有的作品都表达了他渴望实现社会稳定与和谐。
- 洛克在《政府论》中表达的观点对之后全球的政治事件产生了极其深远的影响。这也使得这部作品成为洛克的代表作。

作品的立场

约翰·洛克开始着手撰写《政府论》时早已步入中年。有鉴于其对罗伯特·菲尔莫*的《父权制》进行的批判，作品上篇的写作时间绝无可能早于《父权制》出版的 1679 年，甚至可能直到次年洛克自己购买该书之后才开始撰写。[1] 包括彼得·拉斯莱特（Peter Laslett）*在内的洛克研究学者认为，作品上下两部分差不多是同一时期（1679—1683 年）撰写。这意味着当时洛克是在 47～51 岁。

《政府论》反映了洛克的生活经历以及他参与的政治实践。这意味着这部作品关于政府的理论深深扎根于现实与实践之中，和《论宽容》（*An Essay Concerning Toleration*, 1667-1683）以及《人类理解论》（*An Essay Concerning Human Understanding*, 1689）[2] 一样，成为洛克最重要的著作之一。

托马斯·霍布斯*在《利维坦》中没有像菲尔莫那样凭借圣经经典为王权辩护。洛克对此当然心知肚明。

无论事实如何，和沙夫茨伯里伯爵*等人的来往在很长一段时间里都给洛克贴上了标签，他被认为在君主制*的问题上立场坚定。

《政府论》可以说是洛克在实践政治哲学领域的最后著作。尽管他从未公开承认自己是该书的作者，但没有证据表明洛克晚年曾改变自己的观点。

> "在所有关于财产的论述中，没有比《政府论》这部作品解释得更清楚的了。"
>
> —— 约翰·洛克：《致理查德王的信》，见《洛克文集》

作品的接受

洛克的其他作品中包含了各式各样的观点。这些观点有时和他最著名的论述中涉及的政治主题天差地别。例如，在《人类理解论》中，洛克更关注人类思维探究真理的方式、简单的观念如何发展成为复杂观念，并批判了"天赋观念"论。

如果排除这些论述，洛克作品则构成了一个有机连贯的整体。这是因为他所倡导的理念都和政治稳定、社会和谐有关。即使如此，洛克作品的主题仍然涉猎广泛，包括医学、宗教正统与国家、宗教宽容和自然哲学。[3]

洛克的影响力非一时三刻所形成。有证据显示，直到他逝世（1704）多年后，[4]《政府论》才得到读者的广泛关注。然而，该书逐渐成为美国和法国共和派奠基者们政治思想的主要来源。其中最受青睐的是他关于政府遵守法律而非服从统治者个人意志的观点。这使得这部作品具有"普世性"参考价值。[5]

尽管算不上流传广泛，但洛克的作品在他生前就曾被人们所提及。政治家兼哲学家威廉·莫利纽兹（William Molyneux）*曾提到这部作品是批判绝对王权*的重要论述，认为洛克实现了自己的目标，提供了有说服力的论证。同时代的散文家沃特·莫伊尔（Walter Moyle）*也承认洛克作品的重要性，表示他所写的内容可以说奠定了"政治学的基础"。[6]

作品的重要性

一般认为，《政府论》不仅很好地反映了其所属时代的风貌，其所涉及的政治学观点也能够运用于不同的政治历史语境。18世纪至今的政治思想家们不断提及洛克的观点，这其中就包括参与美国和法国革命*的政治先贤，他们为建立现代民主政府起了举足轻重的作用。[7]由于1689年第一次出版时作者并未公开自己的身份，显然这部作品没有提升洛克的声望。然而早在这部作品之前，洛克就以学者和名门（如沙夫茨伯里伯爵）的私人医师的身份为世人所熟知。

可以说，洛克的权威主要得益于他对政治发展前景的预见性。1775—1783年的美国独立战争便和洛克对政府须为人民负责的观点有部分关系。这场关于理念的交锋也对1789年法国大革命起到了助推作用。*洛克的观点在1788年美国宪法*中被奉为经典。该宪法是世界上最具影响力的政治文件之一，这同时也使得《政府论》成为历史上最有影响力的政治文本之一。此外，洛克还启发了后世许多重要的政治哲学家，包括托马斯·潘恩、让·雅克·卢梭和伊曼努尔·康德。*

《政府论》不仅是洛克最重要的作品，也是西方政治哲学经典中最重要的作品之一。自此之后，自由主义哲学形成了一股不可阻挡之势。20世纪政治理论家弗朗西斯·福山（Francis Fukuyama）*将此称为"全球性的自由主义革命"。[8]

1. J. R. 弥尔顿："洛克《政府论》下篇年代考据"，载《政治思想史》16，1995 年第 3 期，第 356 页。

2. 约翰·洛克：《论宽容》，J. R. 弥尔顿和菲利普·弥尔顿 编，牛津：克拉伦顿出版社，2006 年。以及约翰·洛克：《人类理解论》，肯尼斯·P. 温克勒 编，印第安纳波利斯：哈克特，1996 年。关于洛克作品和传记的联系，详见 J. R. 弥尔顿："洛克生平和时代"，《剑桥洛克研究指南》，V. C. 切珀 编，剑桥：剑桥大学出版社，1994 年，第 5—25 页。

3. 对洛克在《政府论》下篇中关于革命的态度的分析，详见内森·塔科夫："洛克《政府论》下篇和防止动乱的最佳措施"，载《政治学评论》43，1981 第 2 期，第 198—217 页。

4. 马汀·P. 汤普森："洛克《政府论》的接受 1690—1705 年"，载《政治学研究》24，1976 年第 2 期，第 184 页。

5. 详见埃利斯·桑多斯：《以法为本的政府：政治理论、宗教和美国的建立》（第一卷），哥伦比亚：密苏里大学出版社，2001 年。

6. 摘自拉斯莱特："《政府论》概述"，第 5—6 页。

7. 约翰·邓恩：《约翰·洛克政治思想：〈政府论〉的论辩史》，剑桥：剑桥大学出版社，1982 年，第 6—10 页。这些思想家和革命家包括了伏尔泰、乔纳森·爱德华兹、托马斯·杰斐逊等人。

8. 弗朗西斯·福山："历史的终结？"，载《国家利益》16，1989 年夏，第 4 页。

第三部分：学术影响

9 最初反响

要点 🔑

- 约翰·洛克从未公开承认自己是《政府论》的作者。对于其他思想家们所提出的疑问，洛克也从未作出回应和澄清。

- 友人詹姆斯·提雷尔 * 曾试图说服洛克将《政府论》写得更具哲学性，但洛克并没有完全采纳这个建议。

- 从洛克的思想到现代自由主义国家的发展脉络始终是完整且清晰的。

作品的批评

约翰·洛克不愿公开承认自己是《政府论》的作者，考虑到作品发行量有限（即使以当时的标准来看亦是如此），洛克生前受到的回应和批评寥寥无几。

洛克于 1704 年（《政府论》出版五年后）逝世。因此即使他有心，也没有足够的时间对那些批评做出回应。散文家查尔斯·莱斯利（Charles Leslie）* 在作品中（*The New Association*, 1703）公开对洛克的论述进行批判。[1] 莱斯利笃信君权神授论 *，长期支持詹姆士二世 * 和英国国教。洛克的友人兼政治思想家詹姆斯·提雷尔在书信来往中也私下提出了批评意见。针对洛克作品的严肃的评析多年之后才开始出现，如大卫·休谟 * 就认为《政府论》反映了 1688 年光荣革命 * 的原则宗旨。

对该作品的主要批评之一就是洛克所展现的哲学逻辑前后矛盾。在给洛克的信中，提雷尔在《政府论》出版后不下六次建议他对自然法的定义进行补充。*在提雷尔看来，要批判托马斯·霍布斯*（经常被讥讽为无神论者）的论述，这一点极其关键。提雷尔很明白，洛克对于自然法的观点并未排除上帝的存在。但洛克似乎无法（或者说不愿）在这一问题上做出完全清晰的阐释。[2]

就其哲学家的身份而言，洛克时常受到批评，但他作为政治理论家，却因为将政治权利和财产权利联系在一起*而变得声名卓著。不仅如此，他拥护光荣革命，支持议会权力*高于君权*。这在日后被证明是一种可持续的、成功的治理模式，因而进一步提升了洛克的声望。

> "滥用权力有损公民权利，只对统治者一人有利。"
> ——约翰·洛克：《政府论》

作品的反响

洛克似乎对这部作品受到的所有批评都很抵触。由于知晓作者身份的并不多，所以很少有人直接和洛克谈及此书。他的友人詹姆斯·提雷尔对此倒是一清二楚。

提雷尔似乎希望《政府论》能在哲学（逻辑）性上写得更加扎实，从而能更好地反驳托马斯·霍布斯的论述。霍布斯的哲学论辩的基础是生物决定论*（即认定人民不具有自由意志，其行为由人的身体需求所决定）和数学原理。提雷尔认为，洛克保留神学中关于上帝的论述来解释人们一般认知的善恶观不失为良策，但要驳斥霍布斯关于自然状态的非神学论述，这样的论证还不够扎实严谨。*[3]

在提雷尔和洛克两人之间已知的六封来往通信中，洛克试图对自己的观点做进一步解释。但这些解释都没能让提雷尔感到满意。洛克最多只愿意对霍布斯关于人民在国家形成之前无需遵守自然法*的观点进行批判。他告诉提雷尔说，如果这样做还不够，那他情愿"全盘放弃这场论辩"。⁴这就引出了两种有趣的可能性：要么洛克自认不足以和霍布斯直面辩论，要么他志在创造具有实用价值的国家理论而非构建一套严密的哲学理论。

冲突和共识

洛克不愿回应批评，这意味着他并未真正改变其前后立场。他既不会顺从提雷尔等好友提出的善意批评，夯实自己论述的哲学逻辑性，也不会回应那些反对他观点的人士。⁵也许洛克认为他的其他作品已经把自己的观点解释得十分透彻。又或者，洛克认为卷入辩论是件危险的事，因此不愿意承认自己是《政府论》的作者。

无论如何，正如提雷尔认为洛克的部分观点尚需拓展，后世的思想家们也希望进一步发展洛克的观点。但从洛克的思想到现代自由主义国家的发展脉络依然完整清晰。他关于政府和人民之间达成社会契约*的观点具有永恒的价值，只需稍稍修正契约的细节便可以应用于特定的政治语境。例如，美洲殖民危机期间，十三个殖民州*反对不列颠统治。洛克的人民有权反抗暴政这一观点就和这一全新的政治现实完美结合在一起。

洛克为自由主义奠定了理论基础。从他的观点和相关政治实践所能提炼出的逻辑结论便留给后世去评定吧。

1. 查尔斯·莱斯利：《新联盟》，Gale Ecco 资源印刷版，2010 年。

2. 彼得·拉斯莱特："约翰·洛克概论"，《政府论》（第二版），剑桥：剑桥大学出版社，1988 年，第 79—82 页。

3. 同上，第 79—82 页。

4. 同上，第 80 页。

5. 洛克承认自己是《人类理解论》的作者，因此他对大多数批评的回应都为这部作品进行辩护。

10 后续争议

要点 ⚭━

- 对反抗暴政、追求公民权利 * 和政治独立的人而言，《政府论》极具启发性。

- 从政治经济学家到马克思主义者，* 各种政治思想家们都受到洛克的影响。但其中获益最多的是自由主义者。*

- 洛克的思想对提倡限制政府权力和保障个人自由的保守派人士 * 影响深远。

应用和问题

自 18 世纪后期以来，约翰·洛克启发了那些致力于争取公民权利、政治独立以及反抗暴政的人士。许许多多的政治思想家都认同《政府论》的观点。洛克影响了不少思想家，如激进的法国作家伏尔泰、*瑞士裔哲学家让·雅克·卢梭*以及包括托马斯·杰斐逊*在内的多位美利坚合众国开国先贤。

人们甚至造出"洛克派"（Lockean）一词来形容那些认同洛克思考方式的学者。杰出的洛克派学者包括法国政治哲学家孟德斯鸠*。洛克对"自然状态"*做出定义，并将法律视作型塑国家的根基。孟德斯鸠对此深表赞同。[1] 洛克的另一个观点也极具影响力：政治权力中的立法权 * 和执法权 * 应该分立，且前者的重要性高于后者。[2] 美国政治家詹姆斯·麦迪逊（James Madison）*时常被称作美国宪法之父。*他就从洛克的这一观点中汲取了很多灵感。

对这部作品进行深入分析的话，人们可以将洛克对政治思想的贡献归纳为两点。其一，强调政府立法机构的重要性。其二，在描述财产、货币和财富积累等概念如何演变为政治社会时，洛克将经济和政治议题联系在一起。

美国宪法反映了洛克思想的重要性，这也说明上述的第一点具有"普世"意义。这部宪法强调立法和执法权分立，并要求宪政法律须符合"普世"原则。这些原则包括宪法应代表具有"普世"性的真理——即对所有人一视同仁。

从《联合国宪章》(United Nations Charter)*到《世界人权宣言》(Universal Declaration of Human Rights)*，美国宪法影响了不少国际文书的遣词用句。这一点是研究政治经济的重要组成部分。政权要想获得成功就必须以稳定制造（全民）财富的能力为基础。现如今这已成为基本共识。

> "自由给了那位英格兰天才启发，对此我喜闻乐见。当然前提是政治热情和政党之见没有摧毁这份自由中一切宝贵的东西。"
>
> —— 伏尔泰：《老实人》(Candide)

思想流派

无论古今，不同派别的政治思想家们都强烈认同洛克在《政府论》中的观点。

在洛克撰写《政府论》的时代，政治经济学甚至没有独立完整的学科体系。但政治经济学者们也运用洛克的财产、货币、政治责任等理论，分析国际贸易关系与货币汇率。洛克写作该书正值国家之间合纵连横、激烈交锋的帝国时代。如果没有他的贡献，政治经济学很难实现当时的发展。

洛克对财产权*的论述也吸引了马克思主义者的关注。后者将"所有权"理解为由整个社会所共同享有。

但是，我们必须审视自由主义的政治传统才能认识到洛克的真正影响力。为了应对经济全球化*和尊重本土价值之间的冲突，政治哲学家们将洛克的观点（即将宽容和发展视作社会公益）运用于他们自己的理论。个人自由是许多国家身份认同的重要组成部分——至少在自由民主政体中，政权更替的激烈诉求由于定期选举而得到缓解。

尽管洛克的殖民征服有益于被殖民者*的观点在今天看来叫人难以认同，但他提倡更有效地使用土地，运用有效的经济策略为饥寒交迫的人民和社群提供生活必需品的论述却得到了不少响应。[3]有些学者认为人道主义*并非洛克所关注的主题，但参与殖民州行政管理的背景让他能够游刃有余地对此进行论述——尽管和当代的分析语境大不相同。

研究现状

洛克的思想在当代也获得了很多重要思想家的认同，其中就包括政治哲学家约翰·罗尔斯（John Rawls）*和美国政治理论家罗伯特·诺齐克（Robert Nozick）*。前者因研究如何创造更加公正的社会政治秩序而闻名，后者则在洛克观点的基础之上发展了自由主义的社会观。*尽管他们对政府在社会中应该扮演何种角色持有不同的观点，但都认同洛克所说的个人自由、集体利益和反抗暴政——当然，他们对于理论该如何运用于实践的结论差异巨大。

之后自称洛克派的一些学者，如宪政理论家*唐纳德·卢茨

（Donald Lutz）*研究的是政府该如何在制度结构层面发挥作用，致力于为国家宪法修订提供建议。

大多数美国保守派人士也十分认同洛克以及他关于个人自由和限制政府权力的看法。自由派人士也拥护洛克的观点，他们追求极致的个人自由，希望尽可能地限制政府职能（仅限于国防和基本的法令执行）。

所有这些思想家都曾引述《政府论》中的相关内容来支持他们自己的立场。这部作品包罗万象，运用理性的哲学推演而非局限于特定历史语境的论证，因此它的观点能够被灵活地用于解决当代出现的很多新问题。

---

1. 李·沃德：《约翰·洛克和现代生活》，剑桥：剑桥大学出版社，2010 年，第 140 页。
2. 同上，第 140 页。
3. 从人道主义的角度阐释洛克的作品，详见迈克尔·E. 古德哈特："人权问题辩论的起源和普世性：文化本质主义和全球化挑战"，载《人权季刊》25，2003 年第 4 期，第 935—964 页。

11 当代印迹

要点 ⛋

- 洛克认为立法权和执法权必须分立。这被视作防止腐败的重要手段。

- 和其他很多政治理论家不同的是，洛克相信"人性本善"。

- 在美国的许多政治辩论中，辩论者时常会引用洛克的作品来证明自己的观点。

学界地位

现如今人们在阅读约翰·洛克的《政府论》时，有必要思考文本阐释时所采用的后殖民视角。

能否出于人道主义*原因去干涉另一个主权国家*的内部事务？对于此类探讨，洛克的作品提供了参考意见。[1] 在涉及经济全球化*和政治独立性关系的经济议题上，该作的观点同样不可忽视。

就书中提出的观点而言，洛克是希望引发学界对经济（尤其是资本主义经济*）问题的探讨。他担任殖民州政务官的经历，以及在《政府论》下篇第五章中关于殖民统治对公众有利的探讨都能为这一动机提供佐证。

《政府论》开创了强调和定义政治权利而非政治义务的先河。洛克认为政治社会要求大多数公民本能地为社会正常运转而履行义务，他也相信公民能够做到这一点。

一个国家的政治和政府机构能够轻易地镇压政治行动，让财富和权力落在少数特权阶级手中。[2] 就这一点而言，《政府论》颠覆了政治讨论的传统，转而强调个人权利，开创了将政治与经济发展联系在一起进行研究的新范式。

这一转变造成了深远的影响。这部作品也因此被视作自由主义*思想的基石。

支持人道主义干涉以及"宪政治国"的人士也时常引述洛克的政治观点来证明自己的政策和行为具有合理性。洛克关于财产和政治权利的普遍性论述使之备受人道主义者的青睐，他们认为，"当一个国家的公民正面临种族灭绝*或是基本人权受到威胁的情况，那么即使它是一个主权独立的国家，其他国家也应该（甚至是必须）对其进行干涉。"[3]

这种普遍性特征也反映在洛克关于执法权*和立法权*必须分立的学说之中，受到了自由主义宪政思想家们的认可。他们认为这种权力分立是预防专权和腐败的良策。[4]

> "奴隶制对人类而言是多么肮脏、多么悲惨的存在……很难想象一个英国人，更不要说是一个英国绅士，会为之辩护。"
>
> —— 约翰·洛克：《政府论》

和其他领域的结合互动

《政府论》中体现的政治原则直到今天仍在被学界、政治界和司法界反复探讨。

由于司法裁定通常遵循先例（即参考过去发生过的司法判例），从法律维度来探讨洛克提出的诸项原则是非常有意思的。

约翰·马绍尔（John Marshall）*是 19 世纪美国最杰出的大法官之一。他在做判决时常常将洛克的理论作为重要参考。关于破产的问题，他认为尽管人在订立契约时就清楚可能出现破产的情况，但更应该假定人是带着尊重和履行契约的决心才订立合约的。同样的，他曾引用下篇第二章中关于自然状态*的定义，论证民法*的基础是假定人会忠实履行自己对他人应尽的社会和法律义务。[5]

在研究洛克的学者彼得·拉斯莱特*看来，和其他研究政治权利和义务的理论家相比，"性善论"让洛克显得尤其与众不同。[6]

在政治语境中对人性保持乐观主义的态度对像马绍尔这样的人具有重要影响。鉴于其对美国宪法*所做的阐释，这类人一般被归类为"严格的宪法解释主义者"（strict constructionist）——或原旨主义者*（originalist）。

当代讨论

美国的各类宪政辩论是探讨洛克作品最活跃的平台。包括约翰·洛克基金会*在内的一些机构、组织甚至将他称为美国的思想之父。而在支持扩展资本主义和国际贸易、限缩政府权力、减少税收（见于《政府论》下篇第五、七、九章）的保守派*那里，洛克的名字也时常被提及。

另一方面，自由主义思想家们则引述洛克的观点，强调保护少数派的权利，提升社会宽容度，关注公众利益。这些内容在作品下篇的引言和结论部分都有涉及。

美国主要政党和智库都对洛克思想进行过政治性评论。如克莱蒙特研究所发表了一系列学术论文，从保守派的视角来阐释美国宪法和法律。这些研究认为，在美国《独立宣言》*和美国宪法文本背后，洛克是最重要的理论源头之一。这些人引述洛克的初衷是为了替自己在特定的政治和司法议题上所持有的立场进行辩护。

关于"自由"的论述也一直在国际政治领域被反复提及。所谓的"自由主义民主"国家＊在面对所谓的"极权"国家＊时往往因此占据道德高地，指责后者未能对个人自由给予充分尊重。

1. 迈克尔·E.古德哈特："人权问题辩论的起源和普世性：文化本质主义和全球化挑战"，载《人权季刊》25，2003年第4期，第935—964页。

2. 彼得·拉斯莱特："约翰·洛克概论"，《政府论》（第二版），剑桥：剑桥大学出版社，1988年，第120—122页。

3. 更多内容详见迈克尔·E.古德哈特："人权问题辩论的起源和普世性：文化本质主义和全球化挑战"，载《人权季刊》25，2003年第4期，第935—964页。

4. 例如，埃利斯·桑多斯：《以法为本的政府：政治理论、宗教和美国的建立》（第一卷），哥伦比亚：密苏里大学出版社，2001年。以及唐纳德·S.卢茨：《美国宪政的起源》，路易斯安纳州立大学出版社，1988年。

5. R.肯特·纽麦尔：《约翰·马绍尔和最高法院的英雄时代》，路易斯安纳州立大学出版社，2007年，第261—263页。

6. 拉斯莱特："洛克概述"，第120—122页。

12 未来展望

要点 🔑

- 洛克的观点并没有明显指涉他所处的政治现状。这使得他的论述超越了历史语境的局限。

- 《政府论》中的论述（尤其是涉及政治和财产权利＊的部分）仍然具有"普世性"的参考意义。这些观点的价值并不局限于国家内部政治。

- 对于如何构建公正有效的政治秩序，洛克提出的原则仍然具有指导意义。

潜在价值

洛克在《政府论》中论及政权合法性以及财产权时尽力避免涉及特定的历史语境。这意味着如今在探讨这些议题时，这一文本仍然具有重要的指导意义。

洛克的观点在很多领域都得到运用和发展：提升了对医学伦理学的关注，令专利法更多地彰显社会责任，确保公正的劳动报酬。这说明《政府论》在当代社会仍有极大的潜在价值可供挖掘。[1]

这部作品对于思考环境友好型的治理原则也有帮助。在洛克看来，具备合法性的政治权力是能够提升公众利益的，这也被认为是国家治理的典范。例如，洛克将美洲描绘成一片自然纯净的土地。这表明土地的社会效用为全体公民共同享有是必要的。

同样的，洛克关于劳动力的理论对于防止新型的奴隶制＊以及其他类似的虐待行为也有重要意义。

洛克认为身体是属于人自己的，因此劳动生产的成果也应属于劳动者。对于用不足以维持劳动者基本生活的薪酬来换取劳动成果的做法，洛克是反对的。整部作品都隐含着反压迫的主题。正如作品开头所写的那样："奴隶制对人类而言是多么肮脏、多么悲惨的存在……很难想象一个英国人，更不要说是一个英国绅士，会为之辩护。"[2]

《政府论》下篇进一步阐明了为何奴隶制从本质上来说和自然状态格格不入。"这种不受绝对的、任意的权力约束的自由，对于一个人的自我保卫是如此有必要和有密切关联，以致他不能丧失它，除非他的自卫手段和生命一起丧失。"[3]

现如今来看，作品的部分内容可能已没有太多现实意义——尤其是为殖民主义辩护的内容。* 现在一个国家如果违背人的意愿而将主权权威*强加在人的身上，这种行为已不被视作合法的了。同样的，因为缺少对土地进行农业和工业开发的技术和意愿，洛克便质疑美洲原住民*对自己土地的所有权。在这个认为不同群体皆平等的时代，这样的观点听起来十分刺耳。讽刺的是，这样的观点和洛克在《论宽容》中关于社会差异性的论述大致相同。[4]

尽管存在着种种问题，但《政府论》并未失去其影响力，仍然是西方政治思想不可或缺的一部分。

> "哲学家们出于专业兴趣而关注洛克的哲学。但所有人都对如何变得快乐感兴趣，并为此笔耕不辍。"
>
> —— 伊恩·戴维森，《伏尔泰传》

未来展望

当今认同洛克观点的读者数量庞大，包括了各类研究政治学、哲学、经济学的学者，以及政客、法官，甚至普通大众。这些人往往是政治自由派，*强调个人权利和自由，倡导自由经济和政府减少干预，要求在法律规定下保障公民权利和义务的平等。

著名的例子包括政治哲学家约翰·罗尔斯*和罗伯特·诺齐克*。前者以构建公正的社会政治秩序理论扬名学界，而后者则在洛克派观点的基础上进一步发展了自由派*社会观。有意思的是，对于洛克的观点如何运用于政治实践，两个人所得出的结论大相径庭。

洛克的论述（尤其是涉及政治权和财产权的部分）始终保持着普世性特征，避免局限于本国政治活动的讨论。在近代史上，对他国的军事干涉不止一次以人权*遭受侵害为借口。对滥用权力进行武力干涉应被视作合法行为的观点仍然是当今国际关系发展过程中的一个重要因素（《政府论》观点）。

洛克式自由主义国家在国际事务以及国际机构（如联合国*、世界贸易组织*、国际货币基金组织*）中占据统治地位。这说明了洛克思想的价值得到了一些国家的认可。这也意味着他的思想仍有很大的潜力，通过这些机构组织对政治活动施加影响力。

总结

《政府论》是约翰·洛克论述政治和国家权力的起源、目的及界限的集大成之作。它是为数不多的政治学核心著作之一，被认为对自由主义、当代世界事务和依宪法行政*等议题都具有影响力。美国联邦最高法院*所做的判决和主要哲学著作都曾引述洛克的观点。在包括美国《独立宣言》*在内的诸多革命宣言和文本中，也对洛克思想做了概述。

尽管洛克的很多思想是以他人的（部分）学说为基础发展而成，但他将经济、政治、神学乃至医学知识结合成紧密的整体，构建出一套具有原创性的理论。

洛克的观点中最重要的是政治权力源于人民的授权。一旦出现滥用权力、枉顾大众利益的情况，人民可以收回权力。他的论述富有哲学性和抽象性，使得这些观点能够很容易地运用于不同的政治和历史语境之中。他坚持认为政治权力一旦形成，要想保持其合法性，就必须实行执法权*和立法权*的分立，而且必须对人民负责。这样的观点无疑具有革命性。《政府论》不仅深刻地影响了18世纪美国和法国的革命者，也促使人们在革命*成功后创立新的宪政秩序。

洛克的《政府论》在未来很可能继续发挥其影响力。它批判了父权制，*认定政治权力源自人民的授权，赞成保护政治权和财产权。而一旦发生权力滥用，允许创造新的政治秩序来进行替代。该著作的核心内容是对所有公民的社会政治地位一视同仁。随着新的社会和政治问题（如环境问题）不断涌现，洛克提出的政治权力原则将继续发挥作用，为思考如何建立公正、有效、自由的政治秩序做出贡献。

---

1. 洛克理论的实践范例，详见西格里德·斯特克斯："从道德维度看发展中国家的专利和药物获取"，载《发展世界生物伦理学》4，2004年第1期，第58—75页。以及威廉·费舍尔："智慧财产权理论"，载《财产权的司法和政治理论新编》，史蒂芬·R.门泽 编，剑桥：剑桥大学出版社，2001年，第168—200页。

2. 约翰·洛克：《政府论》（第二版），彼得·拉斯莱特 编，剑桥：剑桥大学出版社，1988年，第159页。

3. 同上，第302页。

4. 约翰·洛克：《论宽容》，J·R.弥尔顿和菲利普·弥尔顿 编，牛津：牛津大学出版社，2006年。

术语表

1. **绝对主义（君主专制）**：相信政府的合法性来源于上帝对其存在和统治的许可。因此，所有公民都必须对政府保持绝对的顺从。

2. **美国独立战争**：1775 年至 1783 年，英属北美十三个殖民州和英国爆发冲突。殖民州随即宣布脱离英国统治。

3. **无政府主义**：旨在建立一个没有权威存在的政治体系或国家。最初这个词所要表达的是"没有法律"的状态。之后皮埃尔·约瑟夫·蒲鲁东对其做了重新定义，主张法律是社会中不同的群体自发订立的契约。

4. **威权主义**：指在一个社会中，个体需要顺从权威，尤其是服从政府的权威。

5. **生物决定论**：这种观点认为，人的行为受到自己身体需求的控制，因此并非拥有自由意志。

6. **资本主义**：提倡私有制和利用财产创造附加价值的经济理论。坚信自由市场（而非政府）才是经济发展的原动力。

7. **天主教教徒**：信奉罗马天主教，是基督教中信众最多、历史传承最悠久的教派。天主教的最高领袖是教皇，居住在梵蒂冈。全球大约一半的基督教信众是天主教教徒。

8. **民法**：民法是调整社会中平等主体之间人身关系的法律，而不涉及刑事犯罪和宗教事务。

9. **公民权利**：指在一个政治国家里从公民身份中延伸出的权利。公民权利保护个人自由表达意见和参与社会活动的权利。

10. **殖民主义**：外来人士对本土人口的统治。

11. **殖民地**：被外来人士占领和统治的国家。

12. **公共利益**：约翰·洛克用这个词来描述一个社会中所有人的福祉。

13. **社群主义**：这种思想认为群体的利益高于个人利益。

14. **保守主义**：一种强调保持现有政治秩序和尊重传统的哲学。相比于激进的社会革命，更青睐渐进式的政治改革。保守主义也强调个人自由高于社会责任。

15. **宪政主义**：该政治理论认为，必须遵照制定好的、人人都要遵守的法律来治理国家。一般而言，宪政主义致力于在私有议题上限制国家权力保障个人自由。

16. **《世界人权宣言》**：联合国大会于 1948 年通过决议，要求签约国保障个人人身安全，废除奴隶制及其他对个人权利的侵害，提供政治避难，维护言论自由等一系列基本权利。

17. **《独立宣言》**：由 1776 年 7 月 4 日第二次大陆会议签署通过。宣布英属北美十三州不再接受英国的统治。

18. **去殖民化**：脱离殖民统治的过程。

19. **民主**：指公民直接或通过选举出的代表来施展政治权力的政治系统。

20. **君权神授**：认为是上帝决定了君主的人选。

21. **英国内战**：1642 年至 1651 年间国王和议会之间爆发的冲突。冲突在英格兰造成了极大的政治社会动荡。

22. **英国公民自由**：通过一系列对君主权力的限制所达成的成果，其中最重要的一点是随意征税的权力被废除。公民自由权还囊括了其他一部分英国传统价值，如接受法官审判的权利。

23. **启蒙运动**：亦称"理性时代"，发起于 17 至 18 世纪的欧洲。尽管和科学革命紧密相关，但启蒙运动并没有产生统一的理论，而是形成了一种认为理性高于迷信的普遍立场。

24. **王位排除危机**：1679 年至 1681 年发生的一系列危机。《王位排除法案》由议会推动，旨在阻止信奉新教的查理二世的兄弟詹姆士二世继位为英格兰、苏格兰和爱尔兰的新国王。该法案最终没有获

得成功，詹姆士如愿登上王位，史称詹姆士二世。

25. **执法机构**：政府中负责执行法律的部门。

26. **女权主义**：一种认为男女应该实现社会和政治平等的社会理论。大多数情况下，该理论对男性为主导的社会进行批判。

27. **法国大革命**（1789—1799）：法国历史上一段充满政治和社会动荡的时期，最终导致路易十六被送上断头台，并起草了数份具有过渡性质的宪法。

28. **种族灭绝**：针对特定族裔群体进行消灭的行为。

29. **全球化**：国际融合的过程。这种融合可能采取多种不同形式——经济、政治和文化。

30. **光荣革命**（1688）：指议会和荷兰统治者威廉·奥伦治的政治同盟推翻英王詹姆士二世，使威廉和妻子玛丽二世（詹姆士二世的女儿）成为统治大不列颠和爱尔兰的新统治者，即威廉三世和玛丽二世。作为拥立威廉和玛丽的条件，威廉和玛丽必须接受议会在立法问题上的权威。这代表了英国在宪政发展历史上的重要进展。

31. **人道主义**：强调人性必须以人类的福祉作为最重要的考量。

32. **人权**：所有人都应享有的基本权利和自由，包括了生命权、自由权，以及追求幸福的权利等。

33. **国际货币基金组织**：1944 年成立，现拥有 188 个成员。设立共享基金，接受成员国注资和借贷。

34. **约翰·洛克基金会**：一家美国保守派智库，1990 年成立于北卡罗来纳。该基金会支持减税和减少社会福利开支。

35. **立法机构**：政府中负责制定法律的机构。

36. **自由主义民主**：这种政治体系强调公民权利、不同政党间定期的自由选举，以及坚持依法治国。

37. **自由主义**：自由主义相信社会创造政府的目的是提升社会福祉，尤其关注个人权利的保障。

38. **自由派思想**：这种政治理论认为国家有责任保护其人民和国土，通过警察维安等方式来确保基本的社会秩序。然而，这种思想也提倡应该允许私有市场来满足社会的需求。

39. **马克思主义**：指卡尔·马克思所提倡的政治体系。强调生产资料从个人到中央政府的转移，从而终结资本主义。

40. **君主制**：该制度支持国家应由一名被赋予皇家权威的个人来统治。君主同时也代表了一种政治机构，为国家的其他组织和功能提供合法性。

41. **美洲原住民**：美利坚合众国成立前，17 世纪欧洲殖民者抵达美洲大陆时生活在北美的部落居民。这些人也被称为美洲土著。

42. **自然法**：这种观点认为人类法律来源于大自然的运行法则，因此相信存在着一些永恒的原则，而这些原则是一切良法的基础。

43. **自然权利**：自然权利理论认为人性包含的一部分权利不是来自法律的授权，而是源于自然本身。这些权利"不可剥夺"，因而不能被否定。

44. **原旨主义者（或严格的宪法解释主义者）**：认为在解读和执行法律文本（此处指美国宪法）的过程中应该尽可能遵照其原本的意涵以及法律制定者的意图的那部分法学学者。

45. **议会**：英格兰的立法机构，由上议院和下议院组成。如今，议会是全英国的最高政治权威。

46. **父权君主制**：这种政治制度中君主是最高领袖，只有男性才能掌握和继承权力。

47. **父权制**：父权制认为只有年长的男性才应该掌握权力。这个词经常用于家庭语境，也用来形容由男性掌权的国家。

48. **嫡长子继承制**：财产和世袭头衔由家中的长子或嫡子来继承。

49. **隐私权**：个人有权不将自己生活中的部分情况对外公开。这一概念被运用于实践中，如必须要有搜查令才能搜查一个人的居所。

50. **财产权**：政府制定的法律，涉及个人拥有和买卖财产的权利。许多经济学家相信，稳定可靠的财产权能保障经济的稳定和成功。

51. **新教教徒**：信仰从 16 世纪罗马天主教分裂出来的基督教教义的教徒。新教放弃了原天主教的许多权利和传统，转而拥护更加简化、等级制度没那么严格的宗教体系。

52. **共和主义**：该理论认为一个国家不需要君主统治，权力源于人民，统治者也必须为人民负责。

53. **国家保护责任**：2006 年联合国通过一项原则，认定成员国和国际社会有义务保护人们免受种族灭绝的危害。

54. **黑麦公馆案**：1683 年企图刺杀查理二世及其兄弟兼继承人詹姆士的未遂案件。最终案件策划者受到英国国家公审。

55. **奴隶制**：奴隶制允许将人当做财产，从而可以被当做商品进行交换。

56. **社会契约**：为了保障自身生命和基本权利，特定社会团体同意接受一个统治者（或统治阶级）的管理。这时候便形成了政府。这一理念也暗示如果政府未能履行责任，那么政府权力便失去合法性。

57. **主权法**：法律而非个体（如君主）才拥有最高权力的法律体系。

58. **主权**：一个国家拥有自我管理、免受外部干涉的权力。

59. **自然状态**：思想家们创造出的哲学工具，用来描述政府存在之前人类生活的状态，从而解释人为何建立政府以及政府应该具有何种功能。

60. **美国最高法院**：美国最高的法律阐释权威。有权裁决某些法律是否符合宪法，废除违宪的法令，对疑难案件作出判决，为下级法庭提供判罚先例。

61. **神学**：和宗教信仰或上帝相关的研究或学说。

62. **极权主义**：一个对社会有着（接近）绝对权威和控制的国家政治制度。

63. **联合国**：1945 年二战结束后成立的国际组织，最初有 51 个国家加入，致力于维持国际和平和稳定，发展国家之间友好关系，促进社会发展，提升生活水准和人权。如今，联合国已经拥有 193 个成员。

64. **《联合国宪章》**：该宪章规定了管理联合国以及成员之间关系的基本原则。宪章还进一步对国际权利和义务做出规定。违反这些原则会引发国际社会的外交、经济甚至军事干预。

65. **美国宪法**：美国的根本大法。1790 年由北美十三个独立州签署通过，不仅规定了本国需要建立何种类型的政府，还保证了每一个公民应享有的权利和保障。

66. **国际贸易组织（WTO）**：该组织负责制定国际贸易规则。其主要职能是保证贸易尽可能地保持畅通、自由以及可预测。

67. **第二次世界大战（1939—1945）**：以轴心国（纳粹德国、意大利法西斯和日本帝国主义）和同盟国（中国、英国、美国和苏联）为两大阵营的全球冲突。

人名表

1. **芭芭拉·阿内尔**：不列颠哥伦比亚大学政治学教授。研究领域包括身份政治和政治思想史。

2. **让·博丹**（1530—1596）：法国政治思想家和法律学家，著有《国家六论》，对国家主权理论产生重要影响。他认为主权统治是绝对的、不可分割的整体，但要求统治者（或统治阶层）遵守自然法。这意味着统治者必须遵守其义务，避免未经人民同意而占有私有财产。

3. **查理一世**（1600—1649）：1625年起成为英格兰和苏格兰的国王，英格兰内战结束被议会处决。

4. **查理二世**（1630—1685）：英格兰、苏格兰和爱尔兰的国王。1651年被奥利弗·克伦威尔击败，被迫流亡海外。1660年克伦威尔死后英国联邦终结，君主制复辟，查理二世返回英格兰。

5. **勒内·笛卡尔**（1596—1650）：法国哲学家，现代哲学奠基人。《第一哲学沉思录》被认为是一切西方哲学思想的基础。

6. **罗伯特·菲尔莫**（1588—1653）：英格兰政治思想家，主要作品包括《父权制》（1680），拥护绝对王权。出于这个原因，他声称社会中的所有人都必须服从君主。

7. **弗朗西斯·福山**（1952— ）：美国政治学家。最著名的作品是《历史的终结和最后之人》，将自由主义民主和自由市场经济视作社会的终极形式。

8. **雨果·格罗修斯**（1583—1645）：荷兰哲学家。提出个人具有自然（因而不可剥夺）的权利。他是最早为社会契约理论奠定基础的思想家之一。

9. **大卫·黑尔德**（1951— ）：杜伦大学政治和国际关系教授。他提倡建立更强有力的国际机构，更好地保障人权。

10. **托马斯·霍布斯**（1588—1679）：英格兰哲学家。在作品《利维坦》中提出了社会契约论，因而后世留名。霍布斯提倡政府（尤其是君主制）是避免混乱的"自然状态"的最佳方法。

11. **大卫·休谟**（1711—1776）：哲学家，同时也是苏格兰启蒙运动的核心人物。他的主要思想包括：一切事物都有物质动因，因此可以通过被科学认证了的方法来发现。

12. **詹姆士二世**（1633—1701）：1685年至1688年间大不列颠和爱尔兰的君主。他被怀疑内心倾向法国和天主教。1688年光荣革命中，詹姆士二世被废黜。取而代之的是一个权力被限缩、明确拥护新教的君主。

13. **托马斯·杰斐逊**（1743—1826）：美国第三任总统。作为美国《独立宣言》的主要起草人，他对美国的塑造产生重大影响，并写下了那句英语中的名言——"人生而平等"。

14. **伊曼努尔·康德**（1724—1804）：普鲁士哲学家。他1795年发表的《永久和平论》被视作当代自由主义思想的起点。

15. **彼得·拉斯莱特**（1915—2001）：剑桥大学学者，研究家庭的历史结构。他运用全新的方法来阐释霍布斯、洛克和菲尔莫的作品，因此扬名学界。

16. **查尔斯·莱斯利**（1650—1722）：爱尔兰传教士，积极拥护詹姆士二世，反对威廉三世和玛丽二世继承王位。他还撰写了大量作品，支持英国国教和君权神授。

17. **唐纳德·卢茨**：休斯敦大学政治学教授。主要研究方向包括美国宪政理论和国际语境下的宪法理论。

18. **尼科洛·马基雅维利**（1469—1527）：意大利外交官、历史学家、哲学家和政治思想家，其代表作《君主论》中提出了很多统治者保有权力的方式。一般认为，这些建议暗示了对君主而言"只要结果理想便能使方法的合理性做背书"，即任何能维持权力的行为都是可以被接受的，无论这种行为在道德层面是否存在瑕疵。

19. **詹姆斯·麦迪逊**（1751—1836）：美国第四任总统，开国先贤之一。

他参与起草了美国宪法，支持《权利法案》。

20. 约翰·马绍尔（1755—1835）：1801 年至 1835 年担任美国最高法院大法官。他的见解形成了当今美国司法体系的基础，包括司法复核的原则，即法庭有权裁定法律是否违宪，并以此作为依据废除法律。

21. 玛丽二世（1662—1694）：詹姆士二世的女儿。1688 年英格兰议会邀请玛丽和丈夫威廉·奥伦治（即后来的威廉三世）成为英国的联合统治者。条件是二人必须接受议会和法律的节制。

22. 威廉·莫利纽兹（1656—1698）：爱尔兰哲学家，向洛克提出了一个哲学问题，被称为"莫利纽兹问题"，至今仍然被哲学家们反复探讨。这个问题是：一个盲人如果通过触摸认识了一个球体和一个立方体的形状，那么假如他恢复视力，能否通过视觉观察来区分两者。

23. 孟德斯鸠（夏尔·路易·德·塞孔达，拉布雷德暨孟德斯鸠男爵）（1689—1755）：法国贵族，同时也是启蒙时代的重要政治哲学家之一。在他最有名的作品《论法的精神》中，他提出法律必须是社会自然演进的产物，必须反映社会的习俗和价值。

24. 沃特·莫伊尔（1672—1721）：政治家兼历史学家。曾在议会任职，支持促进贸易和政教分离。

25. 罗伯特·诺齐克（1928—2002）：美国政治哲学家，任教于哈佛大学。他的作品（如《无政府主义、国家和乌托邦》（1974））在约翰·罗尔斯的思想体系之外提供了一条不同的自由主义道路。诺齐克强调个人权利以及避免政府对社会的干预。

26. 托马斯·潘恩（1737—1809）：英裔政治活动家，著有政治手册《常识》（1776），引导北美殖民地民众反对英国统治，继而引发了美国独立战争。他的《人权论》为法国大革命和共和原则进行辩护。

27. 柏拉图（公元前四世纪）：古希腊哲学家和雅典学院的奠基人。雅典学院是西方第一所大学。柏拉图和自己的老师苏格拉底以及学生亚里士多德一起为西方哲学与科学奠定了基础。

28. **约翰·罗尔斯**（1921—2002）：美国道德和政治哲学家。他最有名的观点是作品《正义论》（1971）中提出的"无知之幕"。他认为，如果我们在不知道自己在社会中所处地位的情况下来建构社会，那么我们所建立的社会体系很可能对那些社会边缘人来说是最公正的。

29. **让·雅克·卢梭**（1712—1778）：日内瓦裔哲学家、启蒙运动的主要成员。他的作品对法国大革命产生了深刻影响。《论人类不平等的起源和基础》和《社会契约论》都是现代政治思想的奠基之作。

30. **赫伯特·H.罗恩**（1916—1999）：美国历史学家，研究荷兰以及早期现代欧洲史。他在罗格斯大学工作了23年，直到1987年退休。

31. **安东尼·阿什利·库珀，沙夫茨伯里伯爵一世**（1621—1683）：重要的英格兰贵族和政治家，曾为奥利弗·克伦威尔的共和政府以及查理二世的君主制政府工作。他参与谋划排除詹姆士二世的王位继承权，后来因此被迫流亡海外。

32. **阿尔戈农·西德尼**（1623—1683）：莱斯特伯爵罗伯特的儿子。他是一名共和派，反对查理二世。他同时还是《论政府》的作者。他积极地活动试图推翻王权，后因叛国罪被处死。

33. **约翰·索莫斯，索莫斯男爵一世**（1651—1716）：在威廉三世和玛丽二世联合执政期间英格兰政治家。曾担任的重要职位包括检察总长、大法官，还在安妮女王和乔治一世统治期间担任英国枢密院成员。他的主要政绩包括倡议1707年英格兰和苏格兰议会的统一，并确保1714年登上英国王位的是新教教徒。

34. **詹姆斯·提雷尔**（1642—1718）：英格兰政治作家、约翰·洛克的密友。他批判君权神授思想，最有名的作品是《父权制不等于君主制》（1681），对菲尔莫的观点进行了严正驳斥。

35. **伏尔泰（弗朗索瓦-马利·阿鲁埃）**（1694—1778）：法国启蒙作家，提倡个人权利和政教分离。他在1756年撰写的《论国家习俗和精神》对政治思想看待历史的方式产生了深远影响。

36. **威廉三世**（1650—1702）：即威廉·奥伦治，原是荷兰执政，娶詹姆士二世的女儿玛丽二世为妻。1688年，英国议会邀请威廉夫妇联合执政，条件是他们必须接受议会和法律的节制。

WAYS IN TO THE TEXT

- John Locke was an English philosopher born in 1632.
- In *Two Treatises of Government*, he argues that it was not God who put the king in charge of ruling the country—it was the people.
- Locke's ideas, radical for the time, began the political philosophy known as classical liberalism.*

Who was John Locke?

John Locke, the author of *Two Treatises of Government*, was born on August 26, 1632, in the English county of Somerset. His father, a lawyer, had been a captain in the parliamentarian army during the English Civil War*—a conflict fought between supporters of a monarchy* headed by King Charles I* and supporters of a system of government where power lay in parliament.* Thanks to his position, he was able to send his son to the prestigious Westminster School in London.

From there, Locke went to Oxford University, where he gained a bachelor's degree in 1656. Further study led to a master's degree in 1658, and a degree in medicine in 1674. After university, Locke worked as a doctor for the Earl of Shaftesbury,* an influential politician of the time. Locke also went to France to work as a doctor, and later gained some experience of international trade by working for the English government.

The Civil War in England lasted from 1642 to 1651 and caused many to ask questions about what kind of government was best for the country. Two men in particular, the political theorist

Robert Filmer* and the philosopher Thomas Hobbes,* arrived at a similar answer: only a king could make sure that everyone in society behaved themselves, they believed, and the king was given his power by God—meaning that his right to rule was divine.* Locke disagreed, and wrote *Two Treatises* as a counterargument sometime between 1679 and 1689, when it was published anonymously, mainly because his ideas were so clearly controversial.

In 1683, Locke had himself been implicated in the Rye House Plot,* a plan to kill the current king, Charles II.* Despite being a Protestant,* Charles had some sympathy with Roman Catholics.* Indeed, his brother James* was one. The Rye House Plotters were Protestants who were staunchly anti-Catholic and feared that the country would once more be ruled by a Roman Catholic when Charles died, because he had no heir and as such his brother James would become king. By killing Charles they believed they would be able to halt the return of Roman Catholics to the throne. Locke's involvement had been to arrange accommodation for one of the main plotters. However, the plot failed, and as Charles cracked down on hardcore Protestants, Locke was forced to flee to the Netherlands and to stay there until a new king, William III,* took control of England in what is today known as the Glorious Revolution of 1688.*

What Does *Two Treatises* Say?

Although most countries in the world were then ruled by some kind of monarch, there had been very little thought given to explaining why. The question of where power resided in a state, however, became a particularly important question in the United Kingdom, where there had been bloody conflict over the extent of the king's power.

King Charles I was executed in 1649 and the Civil War had been costly for England as a whole. Because it was a recent memory, it provided an important context for Locke's political work. By the time he wrote his *Two Treatises*, King Charles's son, Charles II, was on the throne, and the old question of how much power the king should have was being asked again.

Some thought the war proved the need for a strong king to keep order. Thinkers like Filmer and Hobbes, for example, were convinced that without a king the country would fall to pieces. Locke begins *Two Treatises of Government* by arguing with Filmer over the origin of kingly power. For Locke, the king's right to rule does not come from God, but from the people he rules. And Locke does not write about what is best for the people of England alone. He couches his argument as universal—that is, as concerning the rights of all people, everywhere.

He uses the language of the Bible, of science, and even of Hobbes, somebody whose opinions he did not share. Locke does not spend much time in *Two Treatises* talking about real history. Instead he turns to an invented, speculative history to explain his view of society.

In his view, people start out living in what he calls the "state of nature."* Society began, he argues, so that people could decide who owned property. The idea of property is important to Locke since he believes that in the state of nature everything was free and nobody owned anything. But if that were true, Locke asks, how did the idea of property come about?

His answer begins with the argument that, once, people could take what they wanted as long as they left behind enough for anyone else that might need it. While human beings were still few in number, this was not a problem. But as land and resources became harder to find, the idea of leaving behind enough for everyone to enjoy was no longer possible. Some people worked hard to make the best use of what they had, Locke argues. A farmer, for example, mixed his labor with the soil to produce more than would grow if the food grew wild—and this was the germ of the idea of ownership.

The problem of property was that anyone could steal it. So laws to protect property from thieves became important. Laws, of course, have to be upheld, and so people needed some form of government to make sure that everyone followed the new rules. For much of human history, this meant having a king who could keep order in society.

Locke's innovation is to describe this as a kind of contract. Although people still had rights, they gave some of them away in return for the king's protection. The king would make sure that people behaved in a respectful way to each other—but, as far as Locke is concerned, that doesn't mean that the king is above the law. The contract works both ways. If the king does not obey the law, then somebody else should rule.

Why Does *Two Treatises* Matter?

Locke's ideas, describing a society different from the one in which most people lived, were revolutionary. He felt that the people should have some say in who ran the country. If a government did not work in the interests of the people, he supported the idea of rebellion against it.

After Locke's death in 1704, many important thinkers, among them the Scottish philosopher David Hume,* expanded on his ideas. By the eighteenth century they were in common circulation. The American War of Independence,* fought by 13 of Britain's colonies* against the British between 1775 and 1783, was founded on Locke's idea that people need not obey a bad government. Many of the men involved in the revolution, among them the political theorist Thomas Paine* and the statesman Thomas Jefferson,* supported Locke's ideas. When the colonies won the war, they created a type of government similar to the one Locke had argued for, where there was no king, where there were elections, and where the government protected people's rights.

Today, these liberal* ideas do not seem controversial. Thanks to Locke, liberalism has become one of the most successful political movements of all time. Notions that started in Europe during the period known as the Enlightenment,* marked by a move towards rational thought, found a home in the young United States, where it was proven that a liberal state would not fall into chaos as men like Hobbes had warned. It was a radical time; in France the people put on trial and executed a king who had, until then, enjoyed something close to absolute power, instituting a republic of their own.

Those living in a liberal democracy* today enjoy a system of government that owes something to Locke's ideas. The influential US Constitution,* for example, a document written to describe and guarantee the rights of American citizens, was based on Locke's philosophy. It continues to be relevant to American politics now.

Today, when people suspect their government is growing powerful at the expense of their liberty—threatening a right such as free speech or privacy, for example—Locke's ideas can still be useful. Although many important thinkers have modified and added to his ideas, it is Locke who is considered the father of classical liberalism. Without *Two Treatises*, the world around us would be a very different place.

SECTION 1
INFLUENCES

THE AUTHOR AND THE HISTORICAL CONTEXT

KEY POINTS

- *Two Treatises of Government* is one of the greatest works ever written in political philosophy and had a clear influence long after John Locke's death in 1704.

- Locke was a privileged member of society and received what was for the time an excellent education.

- An attempt had been made in England to govern the country without a king. Though of limited success, it had been no *less* successful than monarchy had been, and had therefore inspired questions about which system was best.

Why Read This Text?

There is considerable debate over the originality of many of John Locke's ideas in *Two Treatises of Government*. It is, however, generally agreed that his formulation of the evolution of property rights* and their relation to the creation and functions of the state is a major contribution to political thought.[1] Furthermore, his original and influential work on when it is acceptable to rebel against authority had a direct effect on the tumultuous political landscape of the eighteenth century.[2]

Although *Two Treatises* is a work that attempts to justify many of the ideologies and political actions of its time, it does so without completely agreeing with or rejecting any dominant school of thought. It may even be seen as contradictory in its justification of colonialism,* while rejecting tyranny and calling for rebellion against it.³

What is clear, however, is that its influence stretched well beyond Locke's lifetime. As a work that inspired the creation of the American state and influenced key thinkers such as the radical political theorist Thomas Paine,* the philosopher David Hume,* and the political philosopher Jean-Jacques Rousseau,* it remains one of political philosophy's greatest works. Any attempt to understand the evolution of Western political thought is incomplete without an appreciation of Locke's ideas and the ways in which they were later implemented into working political systems.

> "There is land enough in the world to suffice double the inhabitants had not the invention of money, and the tacit agreement of men to put a value on it, introduced (by consent) larger possessions."
>
> —— John Locke, *Two Treatises of Government*

Author's Life

Locke's father was an English lawyer with a small amount of property. He got his son into a good school, where he did well enough to be accepted into Oxford University. At Oxford, Locke studied politics, medicine, and science more generally.⁴ Although well educated and part of the political class, it was his association with more powerful men such as the First Earl of Shaftesbury,* a politician of some influence, that was to define his career.

It is impossible to disentangle the message of Locke's text

from the influences of his social and educational background, and from his circle of close friends and colleagues. The religious and civil conflicts that England had endured from the mid-seventeenth century onwards had greatly destabilized the country. Virtually everyone in the political class was forced to choose sides between the Roman Catholic* and Protestant* Christian doctrines, between republican* and monarchist,* and so on.

Locke's background as the son of a Protestant and his education at Westminster School in London and Oxford University led him to seek a history of the state that explained its origins in nature and society.⁵ This was an account that undermined religious justifications for the legitimacy of the power of a monarch or government. This history of the state would also allow him to justify colonialism and to explain property rights, which were central concerns in a time of imperial expansion and increased capitalism.*

Although Locke never pretended to be consistent in terms of his philosophy, or to belong to any particular school of thought, his association with Shaftesbury substantially colored his view of politics specifically, and of the world more generally. Through Shaftesbury, Locke participated in pivotal events such as the running of the Carolina colony (now the American states of North and South Carolina) and in what historians call the "exclusion crises."* These were the political attempts to prevent the future King James II,* a Roman Catholic, from succeeding his brother Charles II,* a Protestant, to the throne. Locke genuinely seemed to fear that a Roman Catholic king would plunge the largely

Protestant state into renewed religious war.[6]

It seems unlikely that such a text as *Two Treatises* could have been completed by anyone else at any other time. It legitimized the idea of questioning the divine right of kings*—the notion that a monarch's power came from God—in a quite unprecedented way.

Author's Background

The context in which Locke wrote the *Two Treatises* has been intensely debated. While the exact date of the text—understood to be somewhere between 1679 and 1689—is unclear, the historical background itself is easier to define.

England had been without a king for some 19 years after the execution of Charles I,* but the monarchy was restored in 1660. Although the new king, Charles II, was not welcomed by all, towards the end of his reign questions surrounding his eventual replacement came to dominate political thought. Charles II had no legitimate heir, meaning that his brother James II would be king after his death. This was unacceptable to many, as James was dictatorial, refused to cooperate with parliament,* and above all else was openly Roman Catholic.

When Charles II died in 1685, James II did indeed become king—but his reign lasted less than three years. He fled the country in 1688 and the Protestant William of Orange* and his wife Mary* were proclaimed king and queen in his place, in what has come to be known as the "Glorious Revolution."*

This all means that the text's date of publication, 1689, is significant. Questions of how a nation should best be governed were pressing as the rule of James II had failed. Locke, who had himself been falsely accused of conspiring to kill Charles II in what was known as the Rye House Plot,* had been living in exile in the Netherlands since 1683 and did not return until after the Glorious Revolution of 1688, traveling back with the future Queen Mary II herself.

Regardless of whether Locke completed *Two Treatises* earlier or later, its publication in 1689 showed that the political situation in England was far from certain.

---

1. Peter Laslett, introduction to John Locke, *Two Treatises of Government*, ed. Peter Laslett, 2nd ed. (Cambridge: Cambridge University Press, 1988), 101.

2. V. C. Chappell, *The Cambridge Companion to Locke* (Cambridge: Cambridge University Press, 1994), 228.

3. See especially the second treatise, chapter 5 "Of Property" and chapter 18 "Of Tyranny," in Locke, *Two Treatises*.

4. Laslett, introduction to *Two Treatises*, 17–24.

5. Laslett, introduction to *Two Treatises*, 18–22, 40–45.

6. See David Armitage, "John Locke, Carolina, and the Two Treatises of Government," *Political Theory* 32, 5 (2004): 602–627; also Laslett, introduction to *Two Treatises*, 25–44.

MODULE 2
ACADEMIC CONTEXT

KEY POINTS

* *Two Treatises* was one of the first works to investigate the political philosophy of liberalism.*
* Throughout the period known as the Enlightenment,* a time of discussion and increasing rationality, people started to question long-held ideas about the rights of people and the power of the state.
* Locke began to look at ways in which states could potentially be run based on nature and society, rather than on religious notions about kings who had been chosen by God.

The Work in Its Context

The political philosophy of liberalism, which we can trace from John Locke's *Two Treatises of Government*, centers on a specific idea: the rights of the individual.

Since the consensus appears to be that people cannot be allowed absolute freedom to act as they please, it naturally follows that the government must retain certain powers in order to prevent anarchy,* a society where there is no government or law. While the idea of rights and freedoms is today commonplace, this was not the case when *Two Treatises* appeared in 1689. Indeed, many people felt that the king was above the law—though this may have been more the case in France than in England, as the English had enjoyed traditional civil liberties (they were subject only to laws that were agreed for the general good of the community) for some time.

The English Civil War* of 1642 to 1651 had initially been fought over the idea that Charles I* should be accountable to parliament* on the raising of taxes. But holding kings to account was an idea ahead of its time. Ultimately, Locke's views were not put into practice until after the American War of Independence,* which happened between 1775 and 1783. By that time Locke's ideas had been expanded on by thinkers such as the philosopher David Hume.*

Thanks to Locke, questions about property, tyranny, and political rebellion could for the first time be viewed as something more than abstractions. They were questions grounded in actual events that had affected the lives of many, especially in England. At the same time, Locke's highlighting of general principles helped explain how different types of government and political belief interacted with one another. As a result, his ideas were easily applied to contexts quite different from those he personally experienced.[1]

> "This Sovereign is by no means necessarily a king. It can either be one man or an assembly of men."
>
> —— Thomas Hobbes, *Leviathan*

Overview of the Field

Locke wrote *Two Treatises of Government* in a context rife with political revolution* and controversy. Unsurprisingly, he was not the only thinker who had contemplated these ideas. Two important figures, Robert Filmer* and Thomas Hobbes,* had also tackled the same questions, but had arrived at very different answers.

Filmer's great *Patriarcha*, published after his death in 1680, was as much a product of the contemporary political landscape as Locke's work. Set against the background of the conflict between parliament and Charles I that ultimately led to the English Civil War, *Patriarcha* offered a biblical justification for why kings should rule. Filmer cited the model of a family where the father makes the decisions and passes this power on to his eldest son on death.[2] Though Filmer was not the only philosopher to argue in favor of the divine right of kings* (that kings had been chosen by God, and so therefore had the right to make decisions alone), Locke nonetheless singled him out. The first of the book's two treatises was, in fact, written as a direct counterargument to Filmer's ideas.

Hobbes was an altogether different character to Filmer. His 1651 book *Leviathan*, a very important work, was written during the chaotic years of the English Civil War. In it, Hobbes introduced the concept of a social contract,* which held that governments are formed when a social group agrees to be ruled by a ruler or ruling class so that their lives and certain fundamental rights can be protected. This idea implies that governments that do not fulfill their obligations are invalid.

The significance of this cannot be overstated. The social contract can be seen as the root of all modern Western political philosophy. Hobbes, like Filmer, argued in favor of the right of kings, but on practical rather than theological* grounds. Having witnessed the chaos of civil war, Hobbes believed it was the king who had kept order and the rebelliousness of the people that had brought disaster.

The title of Locke's second treatise states that the purpose of the work is to understand the "True Original [origins], Extent, and End of Civil Government." Locke's core ideas concerning the origins of the state, the need to limit the monarch's* power, the need to equate authority with law, and the importance of protecting political and property rights* all reflect these concerns.[3]

This was no direct counterargument to Hobbes, who agreed both that for power to be legitimate it must serve the people, and that the people should be free to act in any way not forbidden by the law.

The two differed, almost exclusively, on practical matters. Hobbes saw the state of nature* as a violent place where life would be "solitary, poor, nasty, brutish and short."[4] The "leviathan" in Hobbes's work was the king, who protected the people both from each other and from themselves. For him, humanity sold its natural rights to the king in return for his protection.

Academic Influences

In assessing John Locke's *Two Treatises of Government*, it is impossible to disentangle its message from the influences of his particular group of close friends and colleagues.

Locke's education and his religious and family background saw him look for a theory of the state derived from nature and from society.[5] His proposals were a serious challenge to those who wanted to legitimize the power of a king or a parliament on religious grounds. Locke's affiliations with Oxford University, and his friendship with the likes of the Earl of Shaftesbury* and the statesman Lord John Somers,* allowed him to exchange radical ideas.

Locke was born in a time of change. The ideas of the ancient Greek philosopher Plato* had dominated European thought for more than two thousand years. But men like the philosopher René Descartes,* a contemporary of Locke's, had begun to challenge and modify this type of classical thought. In this light, Locke's ideas can be seen as an evolution of Hobbes's, inspired both by the events and by the spirit of the age.

The rational spirit of the Enlightenment was highlighting new ideas and inspiring people to question long-established ways of doing things. Locke may well have been arguing for a contemporary form of government in which the nation was governed by a monarch with limited powers, as some of his friends in the government desired. But his ideas were to have long-lasting effects well outside the politics of seventeenth-century England.

---

1. See Richard Ashcraft, "Locke's Political Philosophy," in *The Cambridge Companion to Locke*, edited by V. C. Chappell (Cambridge: Cambridge University Press, 1994), 226–228.

2. See Robert Filmer, *Patriarcha and Other Writings*, ed. Johann Sommerville (London: Cambridge University Press, 1991).

3. Chappell, *The Cambridge Companion to Locke*, 228–230.

4. Thomas Hobbes, *Leviathan* (Ware: Wordsworth Editions, 2014), 97.

5. Peter Laslett, introduction to John Locke, *Two Treatises of Government*, ed. Peter Laslett, 2nd ed. (Cambridge: Cambridge University Press, 1988), 18–22, 40–45.

MODULE 3
THE PROBLEM

KEY POINTS

* At the time *Two Treatises* was written, thinkers were beginning to ask questions about how society should be governed.
* According to the dominant position, explained in different ways by other political theorists, kings obtained their right to rule from God.
* Locke's thinking continued a process that had begun with Thomas Hobbes,* defining the conditions of the contract that society entered into with its leaders.

Core Question

John Locke's *Two Treatises of Government* has an explicit overarching goal, and it could be argued that the aims of the second part, stated in the subtitle, represent this goal best. He wanted to discuss the "True Original [origins], Extent, and End of Civil Government," and he wanted to achieve this by understanding the nature of "political power."[1]

This question of where political power begins and ends, and what it is for, was both the central question in this work and the pivotal question of the time. Indeed, it is arguably one of the fundamental questions in all political thought. The fact that this was the key question of the day helps us understand why Locke was asking the question in the first place.

Disagreement on these matters had led to civil and social conflict throughout Locke's life, so, on a practical level, these questions meant the difference between stability and peace, uncertainty and war. On a larger level, Locke was aware that these issues were not unique to England in the seventeenth century. So rather than simply writing for his own society, he chose to use philosophical reasoning, which potentially gives his work universal appeal.

> *"By this breach of trust they forfeit the power the people had put into their hands, for quite contrary ends, and it devolves to the people."*
>
> —— John Locke, *Two Treatises of Government*

The Participants

The political environment at the time *Two Treatises* was written provoked a debate that reached well beyond arenas of academic or political discussion. Most of these ideas could be split along rational lines of division, such as between Roman Catholics* and Protestants,* or else between those who favored the power of the king and those who favored the power of parliament.*[2]

As we have seen, the two most influential arguments that ran counter to Locke's view both arrived at the conclusion that the country should be governed by a monarch—but for different reasons.

Robert Filmer's* arguments were biblical in nature. Indeed, his line of thought cannot be properly understood outside a biblical context. God gave to the first man, Adam, complete control over his descendants, Filmer theorized. This political power was passed down from father to son through a system known as patriarchy.* Although no unbroken line could be traced, the line was, in Filmer's view, divinely preserved. Only a king could make laws, which meant, by definition, that the king was above all laws.

Thomas Hobbes's* view was far more grounded in reality than Filmer's. For Hobbes, spirituality was not the main issue when it came to government. He was more concerned with the practical necessities of good government. For Hobbes, nature was an unpleasant place to be, and though he borrowed the concept from a prior thinker, the Dutch philosopher Hugo Grotius,* he made colossal use of the analogy to formulate his theory of a social contract.*

The king received power not through God, but through a society that volunteered to abandon liberty in return for protection. The Hobbesian sovereign must therefore be all-powerful, controlling all aspects of society, so as to avoid a state of anarchy* with no government or law where the strong would prey on the weak.

Locke rejects this pessimism about human nature, believing that people can create societies that allow for toleration of differences, encourage material prosperity, and protect individual liberties.[3]

The Contemporary Debate

Political thought moved at a slower pace in the seventeenth century. Locke's views should be seen as a process that began with Hobbes (although, as we have seen, Hobbes also owed some debt to the ideas of Grotius).

Since the first treatise was a direct attack on the ideas put forward by Filmer, this should be seen as an implicit part of the debate. Locke disagrees utterly with Filmer. With Hobbes, on the other hand, Locke is modifying the theory of the social contract to an extent where a different conclusion is reached. Locke's views were, however, not formulated in isolation. Several other writers dealt with many of the same topics and even came to similar conclusions. His friend the political writer James Tyrrell,* for example, wrote a work called *Patriarcha non Monarcha*, which was initially far more influential in contradicting Robert Filmer's* arguments for absolute monarchy.* An even more radical text came from the republican* Algernon Sidney,* whose *Discourses Concerning Government* also went against Filmer.[4]

Although his work derives many of its ideas from other thinkers, Locke combines his theories of property, social evolution, and political accountability in ways that create a cohesive theory of political rights based on universal principles and serve in some ways to justify revolution.* Locke's state of nature,* for instance, expands on Hobbes's ideas of instability and risk to property to argue that the protection of this property actually forms the basis of the social contract between people and their state.

Locke's influence stretched well beyond the seventeenth century. His views became an integral part of the political discourse that included thinkers such as Jean-Jacques Rousseau* and Thomas Paine,* who advocated complete political equality for citizens and who opposed monarchy in favor of rule by fellow citizens subject to the law and to free elections. Impressively, Locke's views have remained influential ever since.[5]

1. John Locke, *Two Treatises of Government*, ed. Peter Laslett, 2nd ed. (Cambridge: Cambridge University Press, 1988), 267–268.

2. For a discussion of the immediate context of the work, see Peter Laslett, introduction to Locke, *Two Treatises*, 45–66.

3. For an interesting account of how Locke viewed colonialism as a means of creating ideal government, see Barbara Arneil, *John Locke and America: The Defense of English Colonialism* (Oxford: Oxford University Press, 1996).

4. Algernon Sidney, *Discourses Concerning Government* (London, 1698), accessed April 7, 2015, http://www.constitution.org/as/dcg_000.htm.

5. See Martyn P. Thompson, "The Reception of Locke's Two Treatises of Government 1690–1705," *Political Studies* 24, 2 (1976): 184–191; see also Ellis Sandoz, *A Government of Laws: Political Theory, Religion, and the American Founding*, vol. 1 (Columbia: University of Missouri Press, 2001).

MODULE 4
THE AUTHOR'S CONTRIBUTION

KEY POINTS

* Locke rejects the idea that a king's power comes directly from God and that the king's subjects owe absolute obedience to him.

* His argument is based largely on the idea of a social contract,* where a social group agrees to be ruled in return for rights that are protected. Governments that do not provide such protected rights are not legitimate.

* Locke's work took existing ideas, but developed both new ideas and new conclusions out of them.

Author's Aims

In *Two Treatises of Government*, John Locke puts forward a number of central ideas and addresses them in a uniquely inventive way. Although he clearly draws on his practical experience of politics, he avoids any actual reference to English history or constitutional law—and this was somewhat unusual for the writing of the time.[1] Considering the political acts and thought of men like his patron and friend the First Earl of Shaftesbury,* who attempted to intervene in the succession to the throne of the United Kingdom, and in Locke's adaptation of Thomas Hobbes's* ideas, it is clear that Locke was working in response to the intellectual and political landscape of his day.

He arrives at his conclusions by first discussing his rejection of the idea that kings are divinely ordained to rule. In a manner consistent with his background as a physician, once he diagnoses the problems, he proceeds to offer improvements or corrections—cures, in other words. Despite building on the ideas of men like the French political theorist Jean Bodin*—whose view of protecting property rights* as part of natural law* placed a genuine limit on the power of the sovereign[2]—Locke distinguishes his ideas by offering solutions with both universal and practical applications. If the text can be viewed as a challenge to orthodox thought, that is testament to the radical ideas it contains.

Although Locke's ideas are often seen as being in the tradition of political liberalism*—which emphasizes individual rights and responsibilities in government, and limits its powers—they are also highly community-minded. This emphasis on the rights of the individual was not commonplace in the seventeenth century. Ideas of democracy* had been refuted by the Greek philosopher Plato* more than two thousand years before, and the reverence which most—though not all—philosophers of this time felt towards classical thought guided, and perhaps even served to stagnate, political thought long after Locke's death.

"The power that every individual gave the society, when he entered into it, can never revert to the individuals again, as long as the society lasts, but will always remain in the community, because without this there can be no community, no common-wealth."

——John Locke, *Two Treatises of Government*

Approach

Locke's use of language reflects the spirit in which he enters into what should be seen as the political debate of his age. His choice of the word "common-wealth," for example, does not simply suggest simply a different name for a state but, rather, a state genuinely concerned with the "common wealth," or well-being of all. Locke goes on to finish the text by stating that when this common wealth is ignored or abused, the people have the right to place a new government in power or even to create entirely new political institutions, "as they think good."[3] If Locke was not advocating democracy as it would be understood today, he was advocating a form of democracy based on individualism, a social contract between the citizen and the political class, and a concern for the common good. This places the work quite firmly in the tradition of liberal political thought.

In the same way, Locke's views that political states begin as a contract to protect property and evolve into systems where law is sovereign (has supreme power), even over the king or queen, was a unique addition to human thought. The execution of Charles I* in 1649, the restoration of the monarchy* under Charles II* in 1660, and the deposing of James II* in 1688 were all fresh memories in England at the time Locke wrote *Two Treatises* and each event marked the triumph of one side of the political spectrum over the other. Locke's views justify the removal of two kings and can be read in two ways—as a genuine call to revolution on the one hand, and as an argument that a monarch could be removed *only* if an abuse of power had occurred on the other.[4] In other words, Locke's arguments could be cited as justification for the major, tumultuous, events of seventeenth-century English history.

It is important to remember that while Locke does not refer to these historical events at all, the subtext would certainly have been understood by those reading the work. His most enduring and unique contribution is still the fact that the text paved the way for a justification of the political actions of the past, while at the same time advocating a new form of future government—strong, fixed-term, and subject to the will of the people.

Contribution in Context

In chapter 5 of the second treatise, Locke writes that there is "land enough in the world to suffice double the inhabitants had not the invention of money, and the tacit agreement of men to put a value on it, introduced (by consent) larger possessions."[5] This leads to his proposition that the invention of money allowed people to acquire more property than they could possibly use and, thus, led to scarcity that would not exist otherwise. In doing so Locke is engaging in a thought experiment, known as a state of nature,* which begins with us asking ourselves to imagine what life was like before the invention of society and the political institutions that belong to it.

Locke's second treatise should be viewed as a form of social contract theory that borrows heavily from Hobbes. But the two men differed significantly on one point. For Hobbes the state of nature was a violent, lawless place where the strong preyed on the weak. Locke, on the other hand, felt that the state of nature was governed by laws, and was not without reason. His contribution, then, was to expand the argument, taking existing ideas and developing new ideas and conclusions from them. Concepts such as the basic goodness of humanity, for example, were absent in Hobbes's argument.

Although such a realization led to the inevitable conclusion that the substance of Locke's work is inextricably linked to Hobbes by way of the social contract, two important caveats must be considered. First, Locke's first treatise is not a continuation of prior thought, but more the dismantling of it. Second, though he traveled the same path as Hobbes, Locke's conclusion is very different. Informed by the social contract, Locke's interpretation takes the reader off on a tangent that ultimately leads to a liberal state.

---

1. For an excellent overview of Locke's career, see J. R. Milton, "Locke's Life and Times," in *The Cambridge Companion to Locke*, ed. V. C. Chappell (Cambridge: Cambridge University Press, 1994), 5–25.

2. For a more detailed list of those who influenced Locke, see Martyn P. Thompson, "The Reception of Locke's *Two Treatises of Government*, 1690–1705," *Political Studies* 24, 2 (1976): 184–85.

3. John Locke, *Two Treatises of Government*, ed. Peter Laslett, 2nd ed. (Cambridge: Cambridge University Press, 1988), 428.

4. For the view that Locke wants to incite rebellion, see Richard Ashcraft, "Locke's Political Philosophy," in *The Cambridge Companion to Locke*, ed. V. C. Chappell (Cambridge: Cambridge University Press, 1994), 226–251. Alternatively, for a view that Locke's motives are unclear, see John Dunn, *The Political Thought of John Locke: An Historical Account of the Argument of the "Two Treatises of Government"* (Cambridge: Cambridge University Press, 1982).

5. Peter Laslett, introduction to Locke, *Two Treatises*, 293.

SECTION 2
IDEAS

MAIN IDEAS

KEY POINTS

* Locke argues that although people give up certain rights in order to live in society, there is a limit to how much power they surrender.

* He theorizes about the origins of political power and tries to make sense of them.

* Locke's old-fashioned language is sometimes hard to follow, but the way he builds arguments logically helps modern readers keep pace with the work.

Key Themes

The main themes of John Locke's *Two Treatises of Government* are a discussion of the origins of political power, its role in organizing the institutions of the state, the limits of state power, and the conditions under which that power can be overthrown and replaced. Within these themes are several other major topics, including property rights,* slavery,* paternal power, and the division of political power.

The emergence of Locke's themes are best considered in two parts. In the first treatise, he follows the arguments of the political thinker Robert Filmer* concerning the absolute power of the monarch.* Filmer traced this power from the biblical account of Adam and his role as father of all humankind. Locke, in a manner reminiscent of Niccolò Machiavelli's* catalog of the various ways in which a ruler can come to power in his book *The Prince*,[1] examines, and then demolishes, all the different claims that Filmer makes for Adam's power and how these have filtered down to the English monarchy.

The second treatise takes up many of these same themes but does so in an evolutionary manner, tracing political power from primitive society and the development of private property and money. It is an approach that allows the reader to fully understand Locke's assumptions about human nature, society, and the state, and what the state was ultimately for. Once these assumptions are defined and explained, he then describes how political institutions should be divided into a lawmaking power and a law-enforcing power, how the leadership of the state can be corrupted, and what society can do to correct abuses of power.

> "No arts; no letters; no society and which is worst of all, continual fear and danger of violent death; and the life of man, solitary, poor, nasty, brutish, short."
>
> —— Thomas Hobbes, *Leviathan*

Exploring the Ideas

Since the main themes center on the question of power, it is possible to define the rights of man as one of the text's key features. Locke does not advocate a free society; instead he envisions a contract between the government and the people.

The first treatise and the second are separate arguments, even if the first supports the second.

In a society as deeply religious as that of seventeenth-century England, Locke's readers would have had to wrestle with the problem of a divinely appointed monarch: if the power of the king came from God, then any limit placed upon that would be in opposition to God's will, a belief known as "absolutism."*

Locke rejects that notion by ridiculing Filmer's belief that a ruler inherits his position from the first man of the Bible, Adam. Locke denies that Adam had been granted any power over his descendants and argues the practical impossibility of tracing proper heirs through history.

Such an observation might well seem superfluous in less religious times. But for Locke's contemporaries it provided the freedom required to consider the specific conditions needed to *entitle* a government. It also allowed for a discussion of the limits of legitimacy, specifically with regard to when it is permissible to change the leadership and the institutions of the state.

This rejection of absolutism is followed by a hypothetical account of how society develops into a political state.

The Glorious Revolution of 1688,* which replaced the Catholic King James II* with the Protestant King William III* and his wife, Queen Mary II,* provided an important—yet deliberately omitted—backdrop to the main theme. If you thought that James had abused his power, then you could point to Locke for a justification of his removal. But you can also see that William and Mary, being subject to the laws of parliament* (as they were), fit within Locke's model of good statesmanship.[2]

The specific relevance of *Two Treatises* to the political events of the day should not, however, be allowed to detract from the central theme's universal appeal. The idea that governments serve to protect property rights, and that their power is granted by the people, leads to one overriding and logical conclusion: what the people give, the people can also take away.

The right to replace rulers when abuses occur remains one of the text's most influential ideas.

Language and Expression

Though Locke's writing can seem old-fashioned to modern readers, he builds on his ideas in a logical and concise way. It should, however, be noted that Locke's first treatise is less accessible. Its reference to Filmer and its detailed biblical analysis assumes a substantial amount of awareness of these other texts on the part of the reader.

Nevertheless, Locke's way of building a case gradually, making sure the parts support one another effectively, helps to offset the difficulties of trying to understand seventeenth-century English. The cohesiveness and comprehensiveness of his discussion have made this text applicable and inspirational to a variety of politicians, students of politics and law, and political theorists.

Locke's property-based analysis of political rights has been especially influential. By coining new concepts such as "commonwealth,"* he inspired the notion of a society where everyone has a stake in its prosperity. Such a powerful idea was more than a radical statement; it inspired debates and even found its place in documents such as the American Declaration of Independence,* which set out the grounds for the colonists'* rejection of British rule, largely along Lockean lines of violation of property rights and personal privacy.* The continuing dominance of the United States and its constitutional* ideas in world affairs has made this particular influence globally important.[3] Indeed, Locke is viewed as the father of liberalism*—even if he did not use the term in *Two Treatises*.

Locke's ideas were complete and logical, but necessarily rudimentary. He was describing an ideal form of government, not imposing rules and regulations on existing ones. It was not until the Declaration of Independence in 1776 and the successful conclusion of the War of Independence* of the young United States that these ideas were put into practice.

---

1. Niccolò Machiavelli, *The Prince*, trans. George Bull (London: Penguin, 1987).

2. For a very interesting discussion of Locke's immediate aims for this work and the Glorious Revolution, see Lois G. Schwoerer, "Locke, Lockean Ideas, and the Glorious Revolution," *Journal of the History of Ideas* 51, 4 (1990): 531–548.

3. For further discussion on American law and Locke, including its international ramifications, see Ellis Sandoz, *A Government of Laws: Political Theory, Religion, and the American Founding*, vol. 1 (Columbia: University of Missouri Press, 2001).

MODULE 6
SECONDARY IDEAS

KEY POINTS

- Locke emphasizes the themes of colonialism* and slavery.*
- The work references the American colonies* with regard to property. Locke argues that Europeans could make better use of the land than the Native American* population.
- Locke's investigation of divine legitimacy and the passing of property and titles to the firstborn son on death could still be relevant today.

Other Ideas

The most important secondary themes in John Locke's *Two Treatises of Government* are colonialism and slavery, which should be placed in relation to Locke's wider argument.

The related discussions of slavery are meant to demonstrate the dangers of the theory of God-given authority—divine right,* or "absolutism."* Locke's belief is that "a man, not having the power of his own life, cannot, by compact, or his own consent, enslave himself to any one, nor put himself under the absolute, arbitrary power of another, to take away his life, when he please."[1]

Here Locke is laying down the groundwork of natural rights,* ideas that would ultimately end slavery as a political institution. As with many of Locke's ideas, he is describing an ideal state. It would take years before it would become a reality.

References to America and its native inhabitants are also linked to Locke's belief that political society is initially created by the need to protect property. He uses this example to prove that his hypothetical ideas about the development of society have some basis in reality. But he also uses it to show that England had a legitimate right to colonize because its utilization of property was more efficient and so more useful to the common good than that of the Native Americans.[2] Unlike Locke's dismissal of patriarchy,* with its reliance on frequent biblical references, his discussion of colonialism is vivid and easy to read. By first demonstrating that people gain a right to property by adding labor to it, he is then able to argue that colonial expansion was a means of adding labor and value to land that was underused, so was therefore a legitimate enterprise.[3]

> "Nobody can give more power than he has himself; and he that cannot take away his own life, cannot give another power over it."
>
> —— John Locke, *Two Treatises of Government*

Exploring the Ideas

In addition to making a case that political power should be limited and based on the common good, Locke's secondary themes can be useful in making a case for interventions in another state's affairs if it can be justified to be in the common interest.

For Locke, property rights were untouchable. So the question of ownership was pressing. While such ideas are central to the work's principal themes, they develop special significance when applied to the specific concerns of the American colonies. The taking of land from indigenous people required no small degree of justification since property, in Locke's view, was sacrosanct.

Students and academics interested in questions of colonial domination and its relation to liberal* political thought, which seem contradictory at first glance, have also used Locke's defense of colonialism and his descriptions of America as keys to understanding this paradox.[4]

While the text is discussed for what it says about individual political and property rights, it can also be important for those who question the very basis of power relationships in society between men and women, and the proper role of states intervening in the affairs of another state.

Slavery is another important theme. In Locke's thorough and systematic rejection of patriarchy in the first treatise, he demonstrates that the Bible itself can be used to justify individual rights and political equality.[5] These ideas seem to flow naturally into questions surrounding the idea of slavery, where Locke feels it is necessary to emphasize the limits of any single person's power.

Overlooked

Though *Two Treatises* is one of Locke's most cited works, overall, and is generally considered to be a foundational text in liberalism and modern political thinking on universal human rights,*[6] the second of the treatises has received the most attention.

Having traditionally attracted little interest, the first treatise is rarely referred to in other major political works. And what little interest there was in Locke's argument against patriarchal monarchy,* and against unconditional political obedience, has naturally ebbed away with time.

His argument about the difficulty of establishing divine legitimacy* on any rational grounds and the potential for abuse of a state's citizens is harder to understand from a modern perspective, where liberal democracies are prominent in world politics. Nevertheless, the ideas of the first treatise have not become irrelevant over time. Such ideas could even have major implications for understanding the effects of present-day authoritarian* regimes.

Thinkers like the historian Herbert Rowen* suggest that the first treatise is neglected in scholarly literature in part due to a lack of appreciation of its dual role.[7] The work is not simply a rejection of Robert Filmer's* theory on the divine right of monarchs. It is also a statement of Locke's own belief that power based on primogeniture* (the passing of property and titles to the firstborn son, or the closest male heir) is fundamentally wrong.[8] In effect, it diagnoses the disease of political thought for which his second treatise offers a cure.

The fact that the first portion of the text, with its detailed use of passages from the Bible, is largely neglected also reflects a long period in which religious considerations were not taken seriously in assessing political values. However, even Western political theorists have begun to consider in a more detailed manner the role of religious belief in forming political ideas. In a similar vein, scholars such as the political scientist Barbara Arneil* have argued that Locke's specific references to America and its native population have been either ignored or misinterpreted. These passages (primarily found in chapter 5) are seen as especially ripe for reinterpreting the historical role of the work in legitimizing both colonial rule and the expansion of capitalism.*9

Human rights theorists such as the scholar David Held,* who struggle to balance advocacy for universal human rights with local customs and morality, have also taken up this type of critique. The trend towards political and economic globalization* has made resolving this tension even more urgent than it was in Locke's time. Why? Because most states are now subject to a variety of international laws requiring them to respect certain human rights internally and to intervene to protect these rights when they are fundamentally threatened in another state.[10]

1. John Locke, *Two Treatises of Government*, ed. Peter Laslett, 2nd ed. (Cambridge: Cambridge University Press, 1988), 284.

2. Barbara Arneil, *John Locke and America: The Defence of English Colonialism* (Oxford: Oxford University Press, 1996), 1–2.

3. Locke, *Two Treatises*, 290–302. See also Arneil, *John Locke and America*.

4. Barbara Arneil, "The Wild Indian's Venison: Locke's Theory of Property and English Colonialism in America," *Political Studies* 44, 1 (1996): 60–74.

5. Locke, *Two Treatises*, 171–195.

6. For example, Michael E. Goodhart, "Origins and Universality in the Human Rights Debates: Cultural Essentialism and the Challenge of Globalization," *Human Rights Quarterly* 25, 4 (2003): 935–964.

7. See Herbert H. Rowen, "A Second Thought on Locke's First Treatise," *Journal of the History of Ideas* 17, 1 (1956): 130–132.

8. Rowen, "A Second Thought," 130–132.

9. See Arneil, *John Locke and America*.

10. See Goodhart, "Origins and Universality."

ACHIEVEMENT

KEY POINTS

- Locke's ideas were seen as very important by later generations. US statesman Thomas Jefferson,* who was the principal author of the Declaration of Independence, named him one of the three most important modern thinkers.
- The American War of Independence* helped give weight to Locke's views about accountable government.
- Some religious thinkers have criticized the book because, by over-highlighting individual rights, it doesn't pay enough attention to a person's duties towards others.

Assessing the Argument

Although John Locke's *Two Treatises of Government* largely reflects the political and philosophical concerns of his time in late seventeenth-century England, it is generally seen as more significant and relevant to political debate now than it was at the time of its publication. In part, this is because the text was discovered and championed by prominent eighteenth-century thinkers such as the philosopher David Hume,* who said that it captured the very essence of the political ideas of its time, and the statesman Thomas Jefferson, who named Locke one of the three most important modern thinkers.[1]

It is possible that not even Locke realized the full potential of his arguments. His work helped explain the tense political climate of 1688 as William of Orange ascended to the throne of the United

Kingdom as William III* after the Glorious Revolution.* Indeed, at the time of its publication in 1689, the English Parliament* had already managed to limit the king's powers. So in some ways Locke was describing a system of government that already existed. Though earlier drafts of *Two Treatises* pre-date the creation of a limited monarchy,* the publishing date corresponds with its existence as a political reality. In this sense, it is clear that Locke set out to justify this new political arrangement.

The will of the people, however, was not truly reflected in this new system. In fact, the vast majority of people had not been granted a say in the running of affairs. Many powers were still invested only in the king, and true democracy* would not arrive in England until many years later. So it is important to understand that Locke was not advocating a democratic society, even if democratic principles can be seen as the logical end point of Locke's social contract.* It took later thinkers like Jean-Jacques Rousseau* to highlight the need for more general participation in government.

> *"We hold these truths to be self-evident, that all men are created equal, that they are endowed by their Creator with certain unalienable Rights, that among these are Life, Liberty and the pursuit of Happiness."*
> ——The US Declaration of Independence

Achievement in Context

Major intellectuals of the Enlightenment* like Hume, Thomas Jefferson, and the political philosopher Charles Montesquieu* all used Locke's *Two Treatises* in various ways. Hume was attracted to Locke's attempts to explain the different categories of knowledge and his nonreligious account of natural law.* He also valued the fact that Locke's work reflected the full political thought of those English politicians who favored a monarchy that was also accountable to parliament.[2] Indeed, ever since the American War of Independence* against British rule in the 1770s, Locke's work has been seen as an authoritative statement of the principles of accountable government that derives from, and is answerable to, the people. With liberalism* dominant in international law after the end of World War II,* Locke's ideas about the legitimacy of the state, intervention, and when rebellion is justified have become even more relevant.

In Locke's time, no one could have predicted that states would bind themselves to international laws, such as the Responsibility to Protect* doctrine of the United Nations,* which requires those who have signed up to it to intervene in states where people's human rights are being fundamentally violated and their lives (or way of life) threatened.

Although the second treatise was written in part to justify colonialism* and European domination,[3] its ideas (especially in chapters 5 and 19) can now be used to explain why states may interfere in the affairs of another sovereign* state when the common good of its citizens is under genuine threat. The rejection of patriarchal* power as a legitimate basis for political power, as seen in the first treatise, has also become an important source of influence for modern feminists.*

Locke is considered a foundational political theorist in the United States. Lockean ideas are often invoked in contemporary political debates there, whenever people suspect that government is growing too powerful or exceeding its proper role in society. This could include objections to new forms of taxation, which are represented by right-wing opponents as theft of private property, as well as advocacy for stronger protections of speech and privacy rights.*

Limitations

Locke's *Two Treatises of Government* is a text that can be reinterpreted in different political and temporal contexts. Whether a king rules because God wills it, and whether he is due unconditional obedience, are not really burning political issues now. But Locke's beliefs that a government must be accountable and that people have the right to rebel under tyranny have seeped into our popular consciousness so much that they are now taken as political truths in liberal states.

Non-Western, non-Christian readers may struggle with the first part of the text. But the rest of *Two Treatises* has inspired resistance movements calling for individual freedoms and political accountability in many different political contexts, from the civil rights* movement in the United States to the rapid process of decolonization* from the 1940s onwards. Where early readers would have seen the discussion of America in the second treatise as justifying colonial domination for the good of the natives, those same natives now cite Lockean ideals of justice based on respect for property and the good of the community.[4]

This reassessment of Locke's liberal reputation is consistent with reactions to the book from the time of its publication onwards. It has always been seen as potentially powerful in its setting out of individual political rights, and yet it seems to contradict itself in its arguments for subjugation and its lack of a consistent source for universal natural law.* The more communitarian* ethos of some non-Western cultures (that is, the understanding that the community comes before the individual) has also led to Locke's work being seen as perhaps putting too much emphasis on individual rights and not enough on political duties. In fact, this critique is also seen in the Western tradition, particularly amongst religiously minded thinkers, who view this individualism as ignoring a person's duty to their fellow human beings.[5]

Despite these limitations, *Two Treatises of Government* may be considered foundational to present-day liberal political thought on sovereignty. It supports the views that sovereignty is derived from the people, and that the right to redress political abuses likewise remains with the people.[6]

---

1. See David Hume, *An Enquiry Concerning Human Understanding: A Critical Edition*, vol. 3 (Oxford: Oxford University Press, 2000), xxxi, 149; see also Peter Laslett, introduction to John Locke, *Two Treatises of Government*, ed. Peter Laslett, 2nd ed. (Cambridge: Cambridge University Press, 1988), 14–15.

2. Martyn P. Thompson, "The Reception of Locke's Two Treatises of Government 1690–1705," *Political Studies* 24, 2 (1976): 184.

3. See Barbara Arneil, "The Wild Indian's Venison: Locke's Theory of Property and English Colonialism in America," *Political Studies* 44, 1 (1996): 60–74.

4. See Arneil, "The Wild Indian's Venison," 60–74.

5. Laslett, introduction to *Two Treatises*, 121–122.

6. See Laslett, introduction to *Two Treatises*, 122. Also Ellis Sandoz, *A Government of Laws: Political Theory, Religion, and the American Founding*, vol. 1 (Columbia: University of Missouri Press, 2001).

MODULE 8
PLACE IN THE AUTHOR'S WORK

KEY POINTS

* John Locke wrote *Two Treatises* toward the end of his life, so it was his last word on political philosophy.
* Locke wrote about many different subjects, but all his works were linked by his desire to encourage public stability and harmony.
* Locke's ideas in *Two Treatises* were profoundly influential in shaping the world's future political events. This makes it his masterpiece.

Positioning

John Locke was well into middle age before he wrote his *Two Treatises of Government*. Considering its attack on Robert Filmer's* *Patriarcha*, the first part of the work could not possibly have been begun before *Patriarcha* was published in 1679, and probably not before Locke purchased his own copy the following year.[1] Locke scholars such as Peter Laslett* argue that the two portions of the text were written during roughly the same period in Locke's life, from 1679 to 1683, meaning that he was between 47 and 51 years old.

The text reflects Locke's life experience and the political struggles he both lived through and participated in. This sense that it is a theory of government thoroughly grounded in reality and practicality is what makes it one of his most important works, alongside *An Essay Concerning Toleration* (1667–1683) and *An*

Essay Concerning Human Understanding (1689).[2]

Certainly, Locke was aware of Thomas Hobbes's* central argument in his book *Leviathan*, which did not justify the power of kings by looking to the Bible, as Filmer had done.

Whatever the truth of the matter, Locke's association with men like the Earl of Shaftesbury* marked him out for a long time as someone who had held strong beliefs on the role of monarchy* in society.

Two Treatises of Government could be considered Locke's last word on practical political philosophy. Although he did not publicly acknowledge the work as his, there is no evidence that he ever reconsidered his views in his final years.

> *"Property I have nowhere found more clearly explained, than in a book entitled, **Two Treatises of Government**."*
>
> ——John Locke, letter to Rev. Richard King, quoted in *Works*

Integration

Locke's other works were an eclectic mix of ideas sometimes far removed from the political subject matter he is most famous for. In his text *An Essay Concerning Human Understanding*, for instance, he was more concerned with the workings of the human mind, how simple ideas could be transformed into complex ones, and discrediting the idea that some knowledge was inborn.

Despite such tangents, Locke's body of work is coherent

because it centers on his encouragement of political stability and public harmony. Even so, the subject matter of his work covers a vast range of topics, including medicine, religious orthodoxy and the state, the case for religious toleration, and natural philosophy.[3]

Locke's influence took some time to build. There is not much evidence that his *Two Treatises* were widely read until well after his death in 1704.[4] However, they became a major source of inspiration for the political thinking of some of the founders of both the American and French republics,* particularly his view that governments should be under a sovereign law* rather than a sovereign individual. This has given the work global implications.[5]

Despite its limited circulation, Locke's work was mentioned within his lifetime. The politician-philosopher William Molyneux* mentioned Locke's work as an important argument against absolute monarchy,* suggesting that Locke achieved his initial aim of making a strong case for his views. Walter Moyle,* a contemporary essayist, also acknowledged Locke's work, saying he had written what could be considered the "A. B. C. of politicks."[6]

Significance

The agreed view is that *Two Treatises* manages both to be very much of its time and yet to offer an account of politics that is general enough to be applied to a variety of political and historical contexts. Political thinkers from the 1700s to the present constantly refer to Locke's ideas, including those who were instrumental in important events like the American and French revolutions,* which helped to establish modern democratic* government.[7] Since he did not admit to having written *Two Treatises* when it was first published in 1689, the book clearly never made John Locke famous. Yet he had established his reputation long before as a man of learning and as a personal physician to important men like the Earl of Shaftesbury.

So Locke's authority really lies in his foresight with regard to how future political events would unfold. The American War of Independence* was fought between 1775 and 1783 in part over Locke's ideas about a government that was responsible to the people. And this war of ideas also inspired a revolution in France in 1789.* Locke's ideas would be enshrined in the 1788 US Constitution,* one of the world's most influential political documents. This makes *Two Treatises* one of the most influential political texts of all time. Locke also inspired many important political philosophers who came after him, including Thomas Paine,* Jean-Jacques Rousseau,* and Immanuel Kant.*

Not only is *Two Treatises* Locke's most important work, it is also one of the most important works in the entire canon of Western political philosophy. Once established, liberalism* as a philosophy proved to be an almost unstoppable force, leading to what the twentieth-century political theorist Francis Fukuyama* would describe as a "worldwide liberal revolution."[8]

---

1. J. R. Milton, "Dating Locke's Second Treatise," *History of Political Thought* 16, 3 (1995): 356.

2. John Locke, *An Essay Concerning Toleration and Other Writings on Law and Politics, 1667–1683*,

ed. J. R. Milton and Philip Milton (Oxford: Clarendon Press, 2006) and *An Essay Concerning Human Understanding*, ed. Kenneth P. Winkler (Indianapolis: Hackett, 1996). For an excellent overview of Locke's works and their relationship to his biography, see J. R. Milton, "Locke's Life and Times," in *The Cambridge Companion to Locke*, ed. V. C. Chappell (Cambridge: Cambridge University Press, 1994), 5–25.

3. For an interesting analysis of Locke on revolution in the second treatise, see Nathan Tarcov, "Locke's Second Treatise and 'the Best Fence against Rebellion'," *Review of Politics* 43, 2 (1981): 198–217.

4. Martyn P. Thompson, "The Reception of Locke's Two Treatises of Government 1690–1705," *Political Studies* 24, 2 (1976): 184.

5. See Ellis Sandoz, *A Government of Laws: Political Theory, Religion, and the American Founding*, vol. 1 (Columbia: University of Missouri Press, 2001).

6. Quoted in Laslett, introduction to *Two Treatises*, 5–6.

7. John Dunn, *The Political Thought of John Locke: An Historical Account of the Argument of the "Two Treatises of Government"* (Cambridge: Cambridge University Press, 1982), 6–10. These thinkers and revolutionaries include Voltaire, Jonathan Edwards, Thomas Jefferson, and many others.

8. Francis Fukuyama, "The End of History?", *National Interest* 16 (Summer 1989): 4.

8. Sawyer, *Seven Military Classics*, 149.

SECTION 3
IMPACT

THE FIRST RESPONSES

KEY POINTS

* Locke never really acknowledged that he had written *Two Treatises,* and he made no clarifications to points he'd made that other thinkers struggled with.

* Locke's friend James Tyrrell* tried to push Locke to make *Two Treatises* more philosophically sound, without being altogether successful.

* The line that runs from Locke's thinking to modern liberal* states is still intact.

Criticism

John Locke was reluctant to acknowledge the fact that he had written *Two Treatises of Government*, and given the book's limited circulation—even by the standards of the day—there was little or no critical response to it during his lifetime.

Locke died in 1704, just five years after *Two Treatises* was published, so he did not have much time to respond to criticism, even if he had been of a mind to do so. The essayist Charles Leslie's* 1703 work *The New Association* rejected Locke's arguments outright.[1] Leslie argued that kings ruled by divine right,* and spent much of his career supporting King James II* and the established English church. There was also some private criticism of the work in letters from Locke's friend and fellow political thinker James Tyrrell. Serious engagement with Locke's work started much later, when thinkers such as David Hume* began analyzing

Two Treatises as a statement of the principles of the Glorious Revolution* of 1688.

One of the main criticisms of the text has been Locke's inconsistency as a philosopher. Tyrrell's correspondence with Locke shows that he wrote to him no less than six times after the work was published, asking him to expand on his definition of natural law.* This was seen as a crucial element that would allow a challenge to the ideas of Thomas Hobbes,* who was often derided as an atheist. Tyrrell was well aware that Locke's views on natural law incorporated the existence of God. But Locke seemed unable or unwilling to fully work out his views on this issue.[2]

Although Locke's reputation as a philosopher has been frequently criticized, his reputation as a political theorist was greatly aided by his linking of political and property rights.* It was further strengthened when his support for the Glorious Revolution's recognition of the supremacy of parliament* over the monarch* was proven to be a sustainable and successful model for governing.

> "The exercise of power beyond right is ... not for the good of those who are under it, but for his [the ruler's] own private separate advantage."
>
> ——John Locke, *Two Treatises of Government*

Responses

Locke seems to have been very resistant to any criticism aimed at the work. As not many people knew Locke was the author, very few could respond to him directly. His friend James Tyrrell, however, was well aware of Locke's secret.

Tyrrell seemed to want to make *Two Treatises* more philosophically sound in order to find a better counterargument to the work of Thomas Hobbes. Hobbes had based his philosophical arguments both on biological determinism*—the idea that people do not have free will, and behave according to the demands of their bodies— and on mathematical principles. Tyrrell felt that Locke's inclusion of God in explaining what people commonly understood as good and evil was desirable, but that it was not strong enough to refute Hobbes's nonreligious views on the state of nature.*3

We know of six letters exchanged between Locke and Tyrrell in which Locke attempts to give a deeper explanation of his ideas. None satisfy Tyrrell. The most that Locke was willing to do was to criticize Hobbes's position that people were not bound to obey natural law* in the absence of the state. Otherwise, he told Tyrrell that he simply "declined the discourse."4 This raises the intriguing possibility either that he did not feel capable of debating with Hobbes directly, or that he was simply more concerned with creating useful theories of the state than he was with creating coherent philosophical theories.

Conflict and Consensus

Locke's unwillingness to listen to or engage with criticism meant there was no real change in his positions. There was no possibility of satisfying the desires of sympathetic readers like Tyrrell for a more rigorous philosophy, nor of answering critics who actually disagreed with him.[5] It may be that Locke considered that his other works spoke for themselves. Alternatively, he may have been so concerned about acknowledging that he wrote *Two Treatises* that he thought it was too dangerous to get involved in major debate.

Whatever the case, just as Tyrrell felt that some of Locke's ideas needed developing, later thinkers also wanted to take Locke's ideas to another level. But the line that runs from Locke to modern liberal states is intact. His idea of a social contract* between governments and the people they serve is timeless. Only the details of the contract needed to be altered to fit specific situations. When the American colonies* objected to British rule during the American colonial crises, for example, Locke's idea that people should rebel against a bad government collided with this new political reality.

Locke should be seen as offering the intellectual underpinnings of liberalism. The logical conclusions drawn from these ideas and their implementation were left to other people in other times.

---

1. Charles Leslie, *The New Association* (Gale ECCO, Print Editions, 2010).
2. Peter Laslett, introduction to John Locke, *Two Treatises of Government*, ed. Peter Laslett, 2nd ed. (Cambridge: Cambridge University Press, 1988), 79–82.
3. Laslett, introduction, 79–82.
4. Laslett, introduction, 80.
5. Locke's primary engagement with his critics was in defense of his *Essay on Human Understanding*, of which he acknowledged authorship.

THE EVOLVING DEBATE

KEY POINTS

* *Two Treatises of Government* has been an inspiration to people struggling against tyranny, demanding civil rights,* and striving for political independence.

* Political thinkers of all kinds have been influenced by Locke, from political economists to Marxists.* But it is liberals* who have drawn the most from him.

* Conservatives* who favor limited government and individual freedom would strongly relate to Locke.

Uses and Problems

John Locke's *Two Treatises of Government* has inspired those struggling for civil rights, political independence, and freedom from tyranny since the late eighteenth century. Political thinkers of many kinds have identified with the work's ideas. Locke influenced thinkers like the radical French writer Voltaire,* and the Genevan philosopher Jean-Jacques Rousseau,* as well as many of the founding fathers of the United States, including Thomas Jefferson.*

The term "Lockean" has even been created to describe people who subscribe to his way of thinking. Prominent Lockeans include the French political philosopher Charles Montesquieu,* who appreciated Locke's version of the state of nature* and his understanding that law was central to the character of the state.[1] Locke's argument that political power must be divided between a legislative* (lawmaking) and an executive* (law-enforcing) arm, with the former being the more important, was also highly influential.² This idea was particularly useful to the thinking of American statesman James Madison,* who is often referred to as the "father" of the US Constitution.*

Long-term considerations of the text generally reduce its essential contributions to political thought to two points. First is the emphasis on the primary importance of government's legislative branch. Second is the connection Locke draws between economic and political issues in his description of how political society developed from earlier concepts of property, money, and the accumulation of wealth.

The first of these points has had global implications because of the importance of the explicitly Lockean elements of the US Constitution. This constitution enshrines the separation of power between those who create law and those who enforce it, as well as the requirement that the Constitution's laws should conform to its universalist principles. These principles were that the Constitution aimed to embody truths that applied universally—to all people.

The US Constitution also influenced the wording of several international documents, from the United Nations Charter* to the Universal Declaration of Human Rights.* This latter contribution is an essential part of the study of political economy and anticipated the way that it is common today for the success of a political regime to be gauged on its ability to generate wealth—preferably widespread wealth.

> "I should be pleased with the liberty which inspires the English genius if passion and party spirit did not corrupt all that is estimable in this precious liberty."
>
> — Voltaire, *Candide*

Schools of Thought

Political thinkers of many kinds—past and present—identify strongly with the ideas in Locke's *Two Treatises of Government*.

Political economists, whose academic discipline did not exist in any proper sense at the time Locke wrote the work, have also applied his theory of property, money, and political obligation to an international regime of trade relationships, currency exchange, and dispute resolution that would have been difficult to imagine in the fiercely competitive imperial era in which Locke wrote.

Locke's focus on property rights* also drew the attention of Marxists, whose understanding of "ownership" is that which belongs to society as a whole.

However, it is to the political tradition of liberalism* that we must look to find Locke's true influence. Inspired by new challenges in resolving the tensions created by globalizing* economies and a renewed respect for local values, political philosophers have applied Locke's ideas of tolerance and development as a social good in their theories. The freedom of the individual is a fundamental part of many nations' identity—in liberal democracies, at least, where the need to rebel has been moderated by regular elections.

Although Locke's willingness to subjugate colonial* peoples

for their own good is frowned upon, his advocacy for more efficient land use, and for the provision of food for the hungry and for communities to be provided with the means to be economically self-sufficient, have been commented on.[3] While some might argue that humanitarianism* is outside Locke's field of inquiry, his colonial administrative background places him comfortably within this discourse, albeit from a very different context.

In Current Scholarship

Prominent examples of more contemporary supporters of Locke's thought include the political philosopher John Rawls,* who is well known for his theories on how to create a more just social and political order, and the American political theorist Robert Nozick,* who advanced a libertarian* view of society based on Lockean values. Although their ideas about the role the state should play in society are not the same, both appeal to Locke's ideas of personal freedoms, the common good, and tyranny—even if they come to very different conclusions about how they apply in the real world.

More recent self-proclaimed Lockeans include the constitutional* theorist Donald Lutz,* who specializes in accounts of how government should work on an institutional level, and has advised states on the formulation of new constitutions.

Most American conservatives would also strongly identify with Locke and his call for individual freedoms and limited government. This even extends to libertarians, who favor an extreme version of personal liberty in which government functions are limited to things such as defense and basic law enforcement.

All these thinkers have made use of those parts of the *Two Treatises* that best support their own positions. The comprehensive nature of the text and its conscientious use of rational philosophical, rather than historical, arguments makes its application to new problems quite flexible.

---

1. Lee Ward, *John Locke and Modern Life* (Cambridge: Cambridge University Press, 2010), 140.
2. Ward, *John Locke and Modern Life*, 140.
3. For an example of interpretations of Locke in humanitarian discourse, see Michael E. Goodhart, "Origins and Universality in the Human Rights Debates: Cultural Essentialism and the Challenge of Globalization," *Human Rights Quarterly* 25, 4 (2003): 935–964.

MODULE 11
IMPACT AND INFLUENCE TODAY

KEY POINTS

* Locke's views that those who make laws and those who enforce laws should be separate entities are seen as an important protection against corruption.

* What sets Locke apart from many other political theorists is his belief that human beings are fundamentally decent.

* Many US political debates see those taking part draw on Locke's work to prove their arguments.

Position

It is worthwhile considering the postcolonial context in which John Locke's *Two Treatises of Government* is read today.

The work has informed recent debates on the question whether it is right to interfere in the affairs of another sovereign* state for humanitarian* reasons.[1] It has also played a role in economic debates about the relationship between economic globalization* and political independence.

Locke intended his ideas to have an economic—specifically capitalist*—resonance. This is revealed both by his professional history as a colonial administrator and by his discussion of colonial domination as a force for the common good in the fifth chapter of the second treatise.

Two Treatises helped to start the practice of emphasizing and specifying political rights more than political duties. Locke assumes that political society will require most citizens to do their duty instinctively for society to function, and he trusts the citizens to meet their obligations.

The political and governmental institutions of a state can easily move to repress political action and to structure opportunity so that wealth and status end up in the hands of a privileged few.[2] In this light, *Two Treatises* altered the balance of political discussion in favor of individual rights, establishing a tradition of linking political and economic development.

Its impact was both global and enduring and for this reason it is considered a cornerstone of liberal* thought.

Those in favor of humanitarian intervention and constitutional* governance also look to Locke's political values to justify their preferred political programs and actions. The universality of Locke's argument for property and political rights makes it an appealing argument for humanitarians who want to argue that states should (and sometimes must) intervene in the affairs of another sovereign state when that state's citizens are being threatened with genocide* or other violations of fundamental rights.[3]

This same universality, combined with Locke's separation of executive* and legislative* power, is appealing to liberal constitutional thinkers, who see this division as one of the best protections against the exercise of arbitrary power and against corruption.[4]

> *"Slavery is so vile and so miserable an estate in man ... that 'tis hardly to be conceived that an Englishman, much less a gentleman, should plead for it."*
>
> —— John Locke, *Two Treatises of Government*

Interaction

Locke's political principles, as presented in *Two Treatises of Government*, are actively debated in academic, political, and judicial circles to this day.

As rulings tend to be based upon precedent (that is, what has happened in previous court cases), legal considerations are especially interesting.

One of the foremost nineteenth-century chief justices of the United States, John Marshall,* often made Locke's theory one of the central elements in his rulings. On matters of bankruptcy, he argued that, although contracts were made with an awareness that bankruptcy could occur, there was a more important assumption that people had the intention and presumption of honoring their commitments. Likewise, he used Locke's description of the state of nature* from the second chapter of the second treatise to outline exactly why the basis of civil law* is this presumption that people will perform their social and legal duties to one another in good faith.[5]

It is this same assumption of fundamental decency that Locke scholar Peter Laslett* notes in his assessment of what it is that sets Locke apart from other theorists of political rights and duties.[6]

This optimism about human nature in a political context must have had a powerful effect on a man like Marshall, who is generally considered to be a "strict constructionist"—or originalist*—in terms of his interpretation of the US constitution.*

The Continuing Debate

American constitutional debates are one of the most active

areas for discussion of the meaning of Locke's work. Societies such as the John Locke Foundation* even name him the US's intellectual father, while his name is prominent in conservative* circles with regard to arguments favoring the expansion of capitalism and trade, a restricted scope for government action, and minimal taxation, as indicated in chapters 5, 7, and 9 of the second treatise.

On the other hand, liberal thinkers cite Locke for emphasizing the protection of minority rights, tolerance, and consideration of the common good, as discussed in both the introduction and the conclusion of the second treatise.

Politically motivated responses to Locke can be seen in major political parties or think tanks such as the Claremont Institute, which produces scholarly papers that support a conservative view of the US Constitution and law. There is overwhelming agreement that Locke is one of the most important theorists behind the actual text of the American Declaration of Independence* and the US Constitution. So those citing him do so out of a desire to persuade others of the legitimacy of their particular position on a particular political or legal issue.

Ideas of liberty are also constantly used in the field of international politics. Liberal democracies* often take the moral high ground when confronting totalitarian* regimes or societies where the freedom of the individual is not respected.

---

1. Michael E. Goodhart, "Origins and Universality in the Human Rights Debates: Cultural Essentialism and the Challenge of Globalization," *Human Rights Quarterly* 25, 4 (2003): 963–964.

2. Peter Laslett, introduction to John Locke, *Two Treatises of Government*, ed. Peter Laslett, 2nd ed. (Cambridge: Cambridge University Press, 1988), 120–122.
3. For further discussion, see Goodhart, "Origins and Universality," 935–964.
4. For example, in Ellis Sandoz, *A Government of Laws: Political Theory, Religion, and the American Founding*, vol. 1 (Columbia: University of Missouri Press, 2001); also Donald S. Lutz, *The Origins of American Constitutionalism* (Baton Rouge: Louisiana State University Press, 1988).
5. R. Kent Newmyer, *John Marshall and the Heroic Age of the Supreme Court* (Baton Rouge: Louisiana State University Press, 2007), 261–263.
6. Laslett, introduction, 120–122.

MODULE 12
WHERE NEXT?

KEY POINTS

* Locke's ideas were not explicitly linked to the political situation of his day. This has helped them remain relevant throughout history.

* The arguments in *Two Treatises*—especially where they touch on political and property rights*—still have universal appeal. They are not just limited to domestic politics.

* Locke's principles still offer good guidance on how to create a just and effective political order.

Potential

John Locke's effort to avoid linking his principles of state legitimacy and property to specific historical circumstances in his *Two Treatises of Government* has meant that the text continues to have a significant role in the discussion of these issues.

Locke's ideas have been developed in all kinds of interesting areas—to improve medical ethics, to make patent laws more socially responsible, and to ensure that labor is more justly compensated. This shows that the text may still find more social applications.[1]

The work may also be useful for finding principles of governance that are environmentally sound. Indeed, Locke's idea that legitimate political power is power that works to advance the common good has been considered a model for governance. His vision of America as a land of natural purity, for example, speaks for the social benefit of lands remaining common for the sake of the greater good.

In the same way, Locke's theory of labor could be significant in combating modern forms of slavery* and similar abuses.

Here, his idea that people own their own bodies and are entitled to the benefits of what they produce clearly goes against paying wages that do not sustain the basic needs of workers. The entire work has an underlying theme of rejecting oppression. As its opening lines state:"Slavery is so vile and so miserable an estate in man ... that 'tis hardly to be conceived that an Englishman, much less a gentleman, should plead for it."[2]

His second treatise further decries slavery as fundamentally unnatural. "Freedom from Absolute, Arbitrary Power is so necessary to, and closely joined with a Man's Preservation that he cannot part with it, but by what forfeits his Preservation and Life together."[3]

There are elements of the text that could be seen to have less relevance today—particularly the sections that justify colonialism.* It is no longer considered legitimate for a state to assert sovereign* authority over people who do not identify with it. Likewise, Locke's portrayal of the Native Americans* as not being entitled to land because they lacked the skills and will to develop it into agricultural or industrial sites makes for uncomfortable reading in an age where different societies are all considered equally valid. Ironically, this view is largely in accordance with Lockean ideas on social difference discussed in his *An Essay Concerning Toleration*.[4]

Despite these apparent difficulties, however, there is no sign that *Two Treatises of Government* is at any risk of losing influence as an integral part of Western political thought.

> *"Philosophers might be professionally interested in the philosophy of Locke, but everybody was interested in happiness, and everybody wrote about it."*
>
> —— Ian Davidson, *Voltaire: A Life*

Future Directions

Current supporters of Locke's text include a wide variety of scholars of politics, philosophy, and economics, as well as politicians, judges, and the general public. They tend to be political liberals,* who stress individual rights and freedoms, economic freedom and noninterference from the government, and equality between people in terms of their rights and duties under the law.

Prominent examples include the political philosopher John Rawls,* who is known for his theories on how to create a more just social and political order, and Robert Nozick,* who advanced a libertarian* view of society based on Lockean values. Interestingly, both come to very different conclusions about how his ideas might be practically applied.

Indeed, Locke's arguments—especially where they touch on political and property rights—maintain an almost universal appeal that is not limited to domestic politics. The abuse of human rights* has been used as a pretext for more than one military intervention in recent history, and legitimate use of force to combat illegitimate abuse of power continues to be a strong motivating factor in how international relations play out.

The dominance of the Lockean form of the liberal state in

international affairs, and in institutions such as the United Nations,* the World Trade Organization,* and the International Monetary Fund,* shows that his thinking is valued. It also means that this thinking still has impressive potential to influence political events via these institutions.

Summary

Two Treatises represents John Locke's most complete analysis of the origins, purposes, and limits of political and state power. It is one of a relatively small number of texts that are seen as foundational to liberalism, contemporary world affairs, and governance founded in a constitution.* It has been referred to in decisions made in the Supreme Court of the United States* and in major works of philosophy, and has been paraphrased in revolutionary statements and documents like the American Declaration of Independence.*

Although much of Locke's thought was derived, at least in part, from others or in response to others, he nonetheless formulated an original theory of the state by combining economic, political, theological, and even medical values into a cohesive whole.

The most important of these values is the idea that political power comes from the people and, more importantly, that it goes back to them when authorities abuse power and disregard the common good. The philosophical and hypothetical tone of his discussion has also made his ideas easy to apply to political and historical contexts other than his own. His insistence that political power, once established, can *only* remain legitimate when it is divided between the executive* (law-enforcing) and legislative* (lawmaking) branches and that it should be accountable to the people has been literally revolutionary. It was a major influence on eighteenth-century American and French radicals and on those who created the new constitutional orders following the revolutions* they successfully fought.

The influence of Locke's *Two Treatises* is likely to continue in the future. This text rejects patriarchy,* locates the origin of political power in the people, champions the protection of political and property rights, and allows for the creation of new political orders when abuses have occurred. At its heart is the concern that citizens are treated as full social and political equals. As new social and political problems like the environment present themselves, Locke's principles of political power will continue to offer guidelines for considering how to create a just, effective, and free political order.

---

1. For examples of these applications of Locke, see the following: Sigrid Sterckx, "Patents and Access to Drugs in Developing Countries: An Ethical Analysis," *Developing World Bioethics* 4, 1 (2004): 58–75; William Fisher, "Theories of Intellectual Property," in *New Essays in the Legal and Political Theory of Property*, ed. Stephen R. Munzer (Cambridge: Cambridge University Press, 2001), 168–200.

2. John Locke, *Two Treatises of Government*, ed. Peter Laslett, 2nd ed. (Cambridge: Cambridge University Press, 1988), 159.

3. Locke, *Two Treatises*, 302.

4. John Locke, *An Essay Concerning Toleration and Other Writings on Law and Politics, 1667–1683*, ed. J. R. Milton and Philip Milton (Oxford: Clarendon Press, 2006).

GLOSSARY OF TERMS

1. **Absolutism (absolute monarchy):** the belief that the government is legitimate on the basis that it exists and rules with God's implicit approval. So all subjects of the state owe the government unquestioned obedience.

2. **American War of Independence:** a conflict fought between 13 of Britain's North American colonies and the British Empire from 1775 to 1783, following the states' declaration that they were independent of British rule.

3. **Anarchy:** a belief in the creation of a political system or an actual state of being where nobody holds authority. Whilst originally the word was intended to convey lawlessness, Pierre Joseph Proudhon redefined it as a stateless society or societies where groups of individuals enter into voluntary agreements so far as the law is concerned.

4. **Authoritarianism:** a society that is best understood as involving submission to authority and the exercise of authority by a government.

5. **Biological determinism:** the argument that people act according to the needs and appetites of their bodies and so do not actually possess free will.

6. **Capitalism:** an economic theory that argues for private or corporate ownership of property and the use of property to create additional wealth or profit. Free markets, rather than governments, are what drive decision making in this system.

7. **Catholic:** a follower of the Roman Catholic Church, the largest and oldest of the Christian denominations. The head of the Catholic Church is the Pope, who resides in theVatican in Italy. Approximately half of all Christians worldwide are Catholics.

8. **Civil law:** a system of law that deals with private matters between people in a society, as opposed to criminal or religious affairs.

9. **Civil rights:** rights based on citizenship in a political state. Civil rights generally protect the rights of individuals to express themselves freely and to participate fully in society.

10. **Colonialism:** the rule of the native population by people from another territory.

11. **Colony:** a country, occupied by settlers from another territory, that is under the control of those settlers.

12. **Common-wealth:** a term used by John Locke to describe the well-being of all in society.

13. **Communitarianism:** a way of thinking that values the good of a community over that of the individual.

14. **Conservatism:** a philosophy that generally seeks to maintain the existing political order and respect for tradition, and prefers political change to occur gradually rather than suddenly. It also emphasizes individual freedoms over social responsibilities.

15. **Constitutionalism:** a political theory that argues that every state should be run according to pre-established rules that apply equally to all citizens. Generally, it focuses on limiting state power in areas deemed to be private concerns in order to allow for personal liberty.

16. **Declaration of Human Rights:** a resolution passed by the United Nations in 1948 that obligates signatory states to protect individual rights to life and security, outlaws slavery and other abuses of individuals, and creates the universal right to political asylum and to freedom of expression, amongst a variety of other fundamental rights.

17. **Declaration of Independence:** ratified by the Second Continental Congress on July 4, 1776, this was a proclamation that Britain's 13 North American colonies no longer considered themselves to be part of the British Empire.

18. **Decolonization:** the process of being freed from colonial rule.

19. **Democracy:** a system of government in which the people exercise power, either directly or through elected representatives.

20. **Divine right of kings:** the notion that it was God who ultimately decided who would be king.

21. **English Civil War:** a war fought between the king and parliament between 1642 and 1651. It led to great political and social instability in England.

22. **English liberties:** derived from a long process in which the power of kings was limited in several important ways, the most significant of which was the inability to raise taxes. Tied into this framework were other traditionally English values, such as the right to be tried by a jury.

23. **Enlightenment:** also sometimes referred to as the Age of Reason, the Enlightenment began in Europe in the seventeenth and eighteenth centuries. Although tied to the Scientific Revolution, the Enlightenment did not constitute a single unified theory but was, rather, a general bias towards reason over superstition.

24. **Exclusion crises:** these began in 1679 and ended in 1681. The Exclusion Bill was a parliamentary attempt to stop the Protestant King Charles II's brother James from becoming the next king of England, Scotland, and Ireland. The bill was ultimately defeated and James took the throne as James II.

25. **Executive:** the part of government that is responsible for enforcing the law.

26. **Feminism:** a social theory that believes that men and women are socially and politically equal. It often, but not always, includes a critique of society as being male-dominated.

27. **French Revolution (1789–1799):** a period of political and social upheaval that culminated in the execution of Louis XVI and the drafting of several transitory constitutions.

28. **Genocide:** the targeted destruction of a particular ethnic group.

29. **Globalization:** a process of international integration. Such integration takes many forms—economic, political, and cultural.

30. **Glorious Revolution (1688):** a name commonly given to the overthrow of English King James II by an alliance of parliamentarians and the Dutch ruler, William of Orange, who subsequently became William III of Great Britain and Ireland, ruling jointly with his wife, Mary II (daughter of James II). The reestablishment of the monarchy under William of Orange and Queen Mary was conditional on their accepting the authority of parliament in making law and marked a major evolution in English constitutional development.

31. **Humanitarianism:** a belief system holding that humanity should be completely concerned with the well-being of the human race.

32. **Human rights:** the basic rights and freedoms to which all people are entitled. These include life, liberty, and the pursuit of happiness, among others.

33. **International Monetary Fund:** the IMF was set up in 1944 and currently contains 188 nation members, all of which contribute to, and can borrow from, a collective pool.

34. **John Locke Foundation:** a US conservative think tank founded in North Carolina in 1990. The foundation is in favor of lowering taxes and decreasing spending on social welfare programs.

35. **Legislature:** the part of government that is responsible for making laws.

36. **Liberal democracy:** a political system that emphasizes human and civil rights, regular and free elections between competing political parties, and adherence to the rule of law.

37. **Liberalism:** a belief that government is created by society to promote the well-being of society. It also focuses on the rights of the individual person as a central concern.

38. **Libertarianism:** a political theory that argues that the state should be responsible for the defense of its populace and territory and for ensuring a very basic internal social order through policing and related functions. It otherwise advocates that the private market should be allowed to serve the rest of society's needs.

39. **Marxism:** the name given to the political system advocated by Karl Marx. It emphasizes an end to capitalism by taking control of the means of production from individuals and placing it in the hands of central government.

40. **Monarchism:** support for a system of government where a state is ruled by a person who is invested with royal authority. The monarch, as an institution, gives cohesion and legitimacy to all the other functions and organs of the state.

41. **Native Americans:** members of the numerous tribes and indigenous peoples living in North America at the time when European settlers arrived in the seventeenth century, prior to the formation of the United States of America. These peoples are sometimes referred to as indigenous Americans.

42. **Natural law:** the idea that human laws ultimately have their source in the way in which nature itself operates and that there are therefore certain timeless principles that are the foundation of all good laws.

43. **Natural rights:** a theory that asserts that all humanity possesses a number of rights that do not flow from any institution or law, but from nature itself. These rights are "inalienable," so cannot be denied.

44. **Originalist (or strict constructionist):** part of a legal school which argues that texts, in this case the United States Constitution, should be read and enforced in a way that is the closest possible to the original meaning and intent of those who wrote it.

45. **Parliament:** the lawmaking body in England, which consists of two houses: the House of Lords and the House of Commons. Today, it is the supreme political authority across the United Kingdom.

46. **Patriarchal monarchy:** a system of government that has a king at its head and where power is held and transferred through males only.

47. **Patriarchy:** the idea that power is rightly held by a senior male figure. Usually used in family contexts, this term also applies to states where males hold the power.

48. **Primogeniture:** the practice whereby property and hereditary titles are passed to the firstborn son or closest male heir in a family.

49. **Privacy rights:** the right of an individual to keep certain aspects of their life private. Such a concept is tied into notions of needing a warrant to search somebody's house.

50. **Property rights:** the laws created by governments regarding individual rights to own, sell, and benefit from property. Many economists believe that stable and firm property rights lead to economic stability and success.

51. **Protestant:** a follower of a Christian denomination that separated from the primacy of Roman Catholicism in the sixteenth century. Protestantism eventually rejected many of the rights and traditions of Catholicism and favored a more simplistic, less hierarchical structure.

52. **Republicanism:** a theory of the state that does not include a ruling monarch and generally claims that power originates from the people and that the ruler should remain accountable to them.

53. **Responsibility to Protect:** a doctrine that was ratified by the UN in 2006, stating that it is the responsibility of member states and the international community to protect people from genocide.

54. **Rye House Plot:** this thwarted plan to assassinate King Charles II of England and his brother and heir James in 1683 led to a series of state trials of the supposed plotters.

55. **Slavery:** a system that allows human beings to be treated as property and therefore traded as a commodity.

56. **Social contract:** the idea that governments are formed when a social group agrees to be ruled by a ruler or ruling class so that their lives and certain fundamental rights can be protected. This idea implies that governments that do not provide these functions are illegitimate.

57. **Sovereign law:** a system where the law, rather than an individual such as a monarch, has supreme power.

58. **Sovereignty:** the right of any nation to govern itself without undue interference from outside sources.

59. **State of nature:** a philosophical tool that allows a thinker to imagine what human life was like before governments existed and so why people created government and what its proper purposes are.

60. **Supreme Court of the United States:** the final authority on legal interpretation in the United States. It has the power to decide whether laws are constitutional and to invalidate those that are not, as well as to rule on difficult cases and to establish legal precedents that are binding on lower courts.

61. **Theological:** relating to the study of religious beliefs or of God.

62. **Totalitarianism:** a political system in which the state exercises absolute or near-absolute control over society.

63. **United Nations:** an international organization founded in 1945 after World War II by 51 countries committed to maintaining international peace and security; developing friendly relations among nations; and promoting social progress, better living standards, and human rights. It now has 193 member states.

64. **United Nations Charter:** a charter that established the basic rules governing the United Nations and the relationship between its various members. It further describes certain international rights and obligations, violation of which can result in collective diplomatic, economic, and/or military intervention.

65. **US Constitution:** the supreme legal document of the United States. Ratified by all 13 states in 1790, it not only set out the type of government the country was to have, but also guaranteed each citizen certain rights and protections.

66. **World Trade Organization (WTO):** this deals with the global rules of trade between nations. Its main function is to ensure that trade flows as smoothly, predictably, and freely as possible.

67. **World War II (1939–1945):** a global conflict that pitted the Axis Powers of Nazi Germany, Fascist Italy, and Imperial Japan against the Allied nations including China, Britain, the United States, and the USSR.

PEOPLE MENTIONED IN THE TEXT

1. **Barbara Arneil** is a professor of political science at the University of British Columbia. Her work is concerned with areas of identity politics and the history of political thought.

2. **Jean Bodin (1530–1596)** was a French political thinker and legal scholar whose *Les six livres de la république* influenced theories of state sovereignty. He views sovereign rule as indivisible and absolute, but requires the ruler or rulers to be subject to certain natural laws, meaning that they must honor their commitments and must avoid taking private property without consent.

3. **Charles I (1600–1649)** was king of England and Scotland from 1625 until his execution by parliamentarians at the conclusion of the English Civil War.

4. **Charles II (1630–1685)** was king of England, Scotland and Ireland, defeated by Oliver Cromwell in 1651 and forced into exile. He returned to England in 1660 when the English Commonwealth ended and the monarchy was restored following Cromwell's death.

5. **René Descartes (1596–1650)** was a French philosopher who is considered the founder of modern philosophy. His book *Meditations on First Philosophy* is considered a cornerstone of all Western philosophical thought.

6. **Robert Filmer (1588–1653)** was an English political thinker whose major works include the book *Patriarcha* (1680), which argues that royal power is absolute. Consequently, he claims that in society all people are bound to obey and submit to the monarch.

7. **Francis Fukuyama (b. 1952)** is an American political scientist whose best-known work, *The End of History and the Last Man*, cites liberal democracy and free-market economics as the ultimate form of organizing society.

8. **Hugo Grotius (1583–1645)** was a Dutch philosopher who introduced the idea of natural, and therefore inalienable, rights of individuals. He was one of the first writers to lay the foundations of social contract theory.

9. **David Held (b. 1951)** is a professor of politics and international relations at Durham University. He argues for stronger international institutions and protections for human rights

10. **Thomas Hobbes (1588–1679)** was an English philosopher best remembered

for his book *Leviathan*, in which he established what is now known as social contract theory. Hobbes championed government, specifically the monarchy, as the supreme defense against the chaotic "state of nature."

11. **David Hume (1711–1776)** was a philosopher and key figure of the Scottish Enlightenment. His main ideas suggested that all things had a physical cause and should be discoverable via scientifically provable methods.

12. **James II (1633–1701)** was ruler of present-day Great Britain and Ireland from 1685 to 1688. He was suspected of being pro-French and pro-Catholic. He was deposed in favor of a limited, and explicitly Protestant, monarchy in the Glorious Revolution of 1688.

13. **Thomas Jefferson (1743–1826)** was the third president of the United States. As the principal author of the Declaration of Independence he had a profound influence on the shaping of the nation and penned one of the best-known phrases in the English language, "all men are created equal."

14. **Immanuel Kant (1724–1804)** was a Prussian philosopher. His 1795 essay "Perpetual Peace" can be seen as a starting point of contemporary liberal thought.

15. **Peter Laslett (1915–2001)** was an academic at the University of Cambridge who studied the historical structure of the family and is also well known for his novel approaches to the works of Thomas Hobbes, John Locke, and Robert Filmer.

16. **Charles Leslie (1650–1722)** was an Irish cleric and controversialist who actively supported King James II and opposed the accession of William III and Mary II to the throne. He was well known for writing essays and books in support of the established Church of England and of divinely ordained monarchy.

17. **Donald Lutz** is a professor of political science at the University of Houston. His research focuses on American constitutional theory and, more recently, on constitutional theory in international contexts.

18. **Niccolò Machiavelli (1469–1527)** was an Italian diplomat, historian, philosopher, and political thinker, most famous for his book *The Prince*. In it, he suggests various ways in which a ruler can maintain power. It is often interpreted to suggest that "the ends justify the means" for rulers, meaning that any action that maintains power is acceptable, no matter how immoral.

19. **James Madison (1751–1836)** was the fourth president of the United States and one of the country's founding fathers. He helped draft the US Constitution and championed the Bill of Rights.

20. **John Marshall (1755–1835)** was chief justice of the US Supreme Court from 1801 to 1835. His opinions form the basis of much of present-day US jurisprudence, including the principle of judicial review, which means that laws can be declared unconstitutional and invalidated by the courts.

21. **Mary II (1662–1694)** was the daughter of King James II. In 1688, parliament invited Mary and her husband William of Orange (later William III) to become joint king and queen, subject to the condition that they would be constrained by the will of parliament and the law.

22. **William Molyneux (1656–1698)** was an Irish politician who formulated a philosophical question for Locke, called Molyneux's problem, which has continued to engage philosophers to the present day. He asked whether a blind man who was taught to recognize the shape of a cube and a sphere by touch would be able to distinguish it by sight, should he ever gain vision.

23. **Montesquieu (Charles-Louis de Secondat, Baron de La Brède et de Montesquieu) (1689–1755)** was a French aristocrat and one of the great political philosophers of the Enlightenment. His most famous book, *The Spirit of the Laws*, argues, amongst other things, that laws must naturally evolve from societies and must reflect the customs and values of those societies.

24. **Walter Moyle (1672–1721)** was a politician and historian who served in parliament as a supporter of increased trade and decreased clergy involvement in the state.

25. **Robert Nozick (1938–2002)** was an American political philosopher who taught at Harvard University. His books, such as *Anarchy, State, and Utopia* (1974), offered a libertarian alternative to John Rawls's system of thought. They emphasized individual rights and the absence of government intervention in society.

26. **Thomas Paine (1737–1809)** was a British political activist whose 1776 pamphlet *Common Sense* helped turn public opinion in America against British rule, leading to the American War of Independence. His *Rights of Man* (1791) was a defense of the French Revolution and of republican principles.

27. **Plato (fourth century bce)** was an ancient Greek philosopher. Founder of the Academy in Athens, the first university in the Western world, Plato, along with his teacher Socrates and his student Aristotle, laid the foundations of Western philosophy and science.

28. **John Rawls (1921–2002)** was an American moral and political philosopher who is most famous for his idea of the "Veil of Ignorance," which was first discussed in his book *A Theory of Justice* (1971). He proposed that, if we consider how we would structure society if we had no idea of our own position in it, we would be most likely to create a system that is as just as possible for those least well-off.

29. **Jean-Jacques Rousseau (1712–1778)** was a Genevan philosopher and member of the Enlightenment movement whose writings heavily influenced the French Revolution. Both *Discourse on Inequality* and *The Social Contract* are cornerstones in modern political thought.

30. **Herbert H. Rowen (1916–1999)** was an American historian of Dutch and early modern European history. He held a post at Rutgers University for 23 years until his retirement in 1987.

31. **Anthony Ashley Cooper, First Earl of Shaftesbury (1621–83)** was an important English aristocrat and politician who held positions under both the republican government of Oliver Cromwell and the monarchy of Charles II. He was forced to flee into exile after conspiring to have the future King James II excluded from the line of succession because he was a Catholic.

32. **Algernon Sidney (1623–1683)** was the son of Robert, Earl of Leicester. He was a republican opposed to King Charles II and author of *Discourses Concerning Government* (1698). He actively sought to overthrow the king and was executed for treason.

33. **John Somers, First Baron Somers (1651–1716)** was an English statesman who served in the government of King William III and Queen Mary II. His notable positions include serving as attorney general, lord high chancellor, and member of the Privy Council for both Queen Anne and King George I. Among his achievements were advocating the 1707 union of English and Scottish Parliaments and ensuring that a Protestant claimed the British crown in 1714.

34. **James Tyrrell (1642–1718)** was an English political writer and a close friend of John Locke. He rejected the idea of a divinely ordained monarch and was well known for his *Patriarcha non monarcha* (1681), which argued forcefully against Filmer.

35. **Voltaire/François-Marie Arouet (1694–1778)** was a French Enlightenment writer who advocated, among other things, the rights of the individual and the separation of church and state. His 1756 work entitled *Essay on the Customs and the Spirit of the Nations* influenced the way political thought looked at the past.

36. **William III (1650–1702)**, also known as William of Orange, was a Dutch prince who was married to James II's daughter, Queen Mary II. In 1688, parliament invited William and Mary to become joint king and queen, subject to the condition that they would be constrained by the will of parliament and the law.

WORKS CITED

1. Armitage, David. "John Locke, Carolina, and the Two Treatises of Government." *Political Theory* 32, 5 (2004): 602–627.

2. Arneil, Barbara. *John Locke and America: The Defence of English Colonialism.* Oxford: Oxford University Press, 1996.

3. "The Wild Indian's Venison: Locke's Theory of Property and English Colonialism in America." *Political Studies* 44, 1 (1996): 60–74.

4. Ashcraft, Richard. "Locke's Political Philosophy." In *The Cambridge Companion to Locke*, edited by V. C. Chappell, 226–251. Cambridge: Cambridge University Press, 1994.

5. Chappell, V. C., ed. *The Cambridge Companion to Locke*. Cambridge: Cambridge University Press, 1994.

6. Davidson, Ian. *Voltaire: A Life*. 2nd ed. London: Profile Books, 2012.

7. Dunn, John. *The Political Thought of John Locke: An Historical Account of the Argument of the "Two Treatises of Government"*. Cambridge: Cambridge University Press, 1982.

8. Filmer, Robert. *Patriarcha and Other Writings*. Edited by Johann Sommerville. London: Cambridge University Press, 1991.

9. Fisher, William. "Theories of Intellectual Property." In *New Essays in the Legal and Political Theory of Property*, edited by Stephen R. Munzer, 168–201. Cambridge: Cambridge University Press, 2001.

10. Fukuyama, Francis. "The End of History?", *National Interest* 16 (Summer 1989): 4.

11. Goodhart, Michael E. "Origins and Universality in the Human Rights Debates: Cultural Essentialism and the Challenge of Globalization." *Human Rights Quarterly* 25, 4 (2003): 935–64.

12. Hobbes, Thomas. *Leviathan*. Ware: Wordsworth Editions, 2014.

13. Hume, David. *An Enquiry Concerning Human Understanding: A Critical Edition*. Vol. 3. Oxford: Oxford University Press, 2000.

14. Laslett, Peter. Introduction to John Locke, *Two Treatises of Government*, edited

by Peter Laslett, 3–127. 2nd ed. Cambridge: Cambridge University Press, 1988.

15. Leslie, Charles. *The New Association*. Gale ECCO, Print Editions, 2010.

16. Locke, John. *An Essay Concerning Human Understanding*. Edited by Kenneth P. Winkler. Indianapolis: Hackett, 1996.

原书作者简介

英国政治哲学家约翰·洛克（John Locke）是启蒙时代最重要的思想家之一。1632 年出生于一个富裕家庭的他先后为不少社会显要人士以及英国政府工作。他提出的"天赋人权"和政府合法性的观点对西方政治与哲学思想产生了重大影响。洛克终身未娶，膝下无子。他于 1704 年逝世，享年 72 岁。

本书作者简介

杰里米·克莱德斯蒂（Jeremy Kleidosty）获圣安德鲁斯大学国际关系专业博士学位。目前是芬兰于韦斯屈莱大学的博士后研究员，著有《文明的交响乐：西方与伊斯兰立宪主义的共同本源》。

伊恩·杰克逊（Ian Jackson）现在兰卡斯特大学政治哲学与宗教系攻读博士学位。研究方向为新媒体在思想传播中发挥的作用。

世界名著中的批判性思维

《世界思想宝库钥匙丛书》致力于深入浅出地阐释全世界著名思想家的观点，不论是谁、在何处都能了解到，从而推进批判性思维发展。

《世界思想宝库钥匙丛书》与世界顶尖大学的一流学者合作，为一系列学科中最有影响的著作推出新的分析文本，介绍其观点和影响。在这一不断扩展的系列中，每种选入的著作都代表了历经时间考验的思想典范。通过为这些著作提供必要背景、揭示原作者的学术渊源以及说明这些著作所产生的影响，本系列图书希望让读者以新视角看待这些划时代的经典之作。读者应学会思考、运用并挑战这些著作中的观点，而不是简单接受它们。

ABOUT THE AUTHOR OF THE ORIGINAL WORK

English political philosopher **John Locke** is considered one of the most important thinkers of the Enlightenment era. Born into a well-off English family in 1632, he rose to work for a series of highly influential men, and even the government. His ideas about men's inalienable rights and what makes for a legitimate government have had a profound impact on Western political and philosophical thinking. Locke never married or had children, and died in 1704 at the age of 72.

ABOUT THE AUTHOR OF THE ANALYSIS

Dr Jeremy Kleidosty received his PhD in international relations from the University of St Andrews. He is currently a postdoctoral fellow at the University of Jväskylä, and is the author of *The Concert of Civilizations: The Common Roots of Western and Islamic Constitutionalism.*

Ian Jackson is a PhD student in the Politics, Philosophy and Religion department at Lancaster University. He is interested in the role new media plays in the dissemination of ideas.

ABOUT MACAT
GREAT WORKS FOR CRITICAL THINKING

Macat is focused on making the ideas of the world's great thinkers accessible and comprehensible to everybody, everywhere, in ways that promote the development of enhanced critical thinking skills.

It works with leading academics from the world's top universities to produce new analyses that focus on the ideas and the impact of the most influential works ever written across a wide variety of academic disciplines. Each of the works that sit at the heart of its growing library is an enduring example of great thinking. But by setting them in context — and looking at the influences that shaped their authors, as well as the responses they provoked — Macat encourages readers to look at these classics and game-changers with fresh eyes. Readers learn to think, engage and challenge their ideas, rather than simply accepting them.

批判性思维与《政府论》

首要批判性思维技能：评价
次要批判性思维技能：论证

　　约翰·洛克于 1689 年出版的《政府论》是政治理论史上极其重要的一部著作——对现代政治、美国宪法，乃至当代政治实践产生了深远影响。

　　《政府论》不仅对政府的本质及合法性做出了创新性解释，同时也淋漓尽致地展现了批判性思维的两项核心能力：评价与论证。评价指的是对论述是否成立作出判断和评定——主要考察论据的关联性、充分性和说服力。洛克的《政府论》上篇就是评价性的：该卷的核心内容是对罗伯特·菲尔莫爵士的《父权制》进行详细且深刻的解析。菲尔莫的作品以《圣经》内容作为依据，替"君权神授"学说做辩护，认为君主的权威源之于天，神圣不可侵犯。洛克选择照方抓药，同样参考《圣经》和历史记录，对菲尔莫的论述逐条批驳。在揭示菲尔莫的论据要么充分性不足要么根本站不住脚后，洛克得出结论认为前者关于父权制合理性的论述薄弱，没有说服力。

　　在《政府论》下篇中，作者进一步就君权的合法性来源及其本质提出了自己的观点。通过分析处于"自然状态"的人的理性考量，洛克构建了一套具有说服力的论述：文明社会存在的基础是天赋人权与社会契约。

CRITICAL THINKING AND *TWO TREATISES OF GOVERNMENT*

- Primary critical thinking skill: EVALUATION
- Secondary critical thinking skill: REASONING

John Locke's 1689 *Two Treatises of Government* is a key text in the history of political theory—one whose influence remains marked on modern politics, the American Constitution and beyond.

Two Treatises is more than a seminal work on the nature and legitimacy of government. It is also a masterclass in two key critical thinking skills: evaluation and reasoning. Evaluation is all about judging and assessing arguments—asking how relevant, adequate and convincing they are. And, at its heart, the first of Locke's two treatises is pure evaluation: a long and incisive dissection of a treatise on the arguments in Sir Robert Filmer's *Patriarcha*. Filmer's book had defended the doctrine that kings were absolute rulers whose legitimacy came directly from God (the so-called "divine right of kings"), basing his arguments on Biblical explanations and evidence. Locke carefully rebutted Filmer's arguments, on their own terms, by reference to both the Bible and to recorded history. Finding Filmer's evidence either to be insufficient or unacceptable, Locke concluded that his argument for patriarchy was weak to the point of invalidity.

In the second of Locke's treatises, the author goes on to construct his own argument concerning the sources of legitimate power, and the nature of that power. Carefully building his own argument from a logical consideration of man in "the state of nature", Locke creates a convincing argument that civilised society should be based on natural human rights and the social contract.

《世界思想宝库钥匙丛书》简介

《世界思想宝库钥匙丛书》致力于为一系列在各领域产生重大影响的人文社科类经典著作提供独特的学术探讨。每一本读物都不仅仅是原经典著作的内容摘要，而是介绍并深入研究原经典著作的学术渊源、主要观点和历史影响。这一丛书的目的是提供一套学习资料，以促进读者掌握批判性思维，从而更全面、深刻地去理解重要思想。

每一本读物分为3个部分：学术渊源、学术思想和学术影响，每个部分下有4个小节。这些章节旨在从各个方面研究原经典著作及其反响。

由于独特的体例，每一本读物不但易于阅读，而且另有一项优点：所有读物的编排体例相同，读者在进行某个知识层面的调查或研究时可交叉参阅多本该丛书中的相关读物，从而开启跨领域研究的路径。

为了方便阅读，每本读物最后还列出了术语表和人名表（在书中则以星号＊标记），此外还有参考文献。

《世界思想宝库钥匙丛书》与剑桥大学合作，理清了批判性思维的要点，即如何通过6种技能来进行有效思考。其中3种技能让我们能够理解问题，另3种技能让我们有能力解决问题。这6种技能合称为"批判性思维PACIER模式"，它们是：

分析：了解如何建立一个观点；

评估：研究一个观点的优点和缺点；

阐释：对意义所产生的问题加以理解；

创造性思维：提出新的见解，发现新的联系；

解决问题：提出切实有效的解决办法；

理性化思维：创建有说服力的观点。

THE MACAT LIBRARY

The Macat Library is a series of unique academic explorations of seminal works in the humanities and social sciences — books and papers that have had a significant and widely recognised impact on their disciplines. It has been created to serve as much more than just a summary of what lies between the covers of a great book. It illuminates and explores the influences on, ideas of, and impact of that book. Our goal is to offer a learning resource that encourages critical thinking and fosters a better, deeper understanding of important ideas.

Each publication is divided into three Sections: Influences, Ideas, and Impact. Each Section has four Modules. These explore every important facet of the work, and the responses to it.

This Section-Module structure makes a Macat Library book easy to use, but it has another important feature. Because each Macat book is written to the same format, it is possible (and encouraged!) to cross-reference multiple Macat books along the same lines of inquiry or research. This allows the reader to open up interesting interdisciplinary pathways.

To further aid your reading, lists of glossary terms and people mentioned are included at the end of this book (these are indicated by an asterisk [*] throughout) — as well as a list of works cited.

Macat has worked with the University of Cambridge to identify the elements of critical thinking and understand the ways in which six different skills combine to enable effective thinking.

Three allow us to fully understand a problem; three more give us the tools to solve it. Together, these six skills make up the PACIER model of critical thinking. They are:

ANALYSIS — understanding how an argument is built
EVALUATION — exploring the strengths and weaknesses of an argument
INTERPRETATION — understanding issues of meaning
CREATIVE THINKING — coming up with new ideas and fresh connections
PROBLEM-SOLVING — producing strong solutions
REASONING — creating strong arguments

"《世界思想宝库钥匙丛书》提供了独一无二的跨学科学习和研究工具。它介绍那些革新了各自学科研究的经典著作，还邀请全世界一流专家和教育机构进行严谨的分析，为每位读者打开世界顶级教育的大门。"

—— 安德烈亚斯·施莱歇尔，
经济合作与发展组织教育与技能司司长

"《世界思想宝库钥匙丛书》直面大学教育的巨大挑战……他们组建了一支精干而活跃的学者队伍，来推出在研究广度上颇具新意的教学材料。"

—— 布罗尔斯教授、勋爵，剑桥大学前校长

"《世界思想宝库钥匙丛书》的愿景令人赞叹。它通过分析和阐释那些曾深刻影响人类思想以及社会、经济发展的经典文本，提供了新的学习方法。它推动批判性思维，这对于任何社会和经济体来说都是至关重要的。这就是未来的学习方法。"

—— 查尔斯·克拉克阁下，英国前教育大臣

"对于那些影响了各自领域的著作，《世界思想宝库钥匙丛书》能让人们立即了解到围绕那些著作展开的评论性言论，这让该系列图书成为在这些领域从事研究的师生们不可或缺的资源。"

—— 威廉·特朗佐教授，加利福尼亚大学圣地亚哥分校

"Macat offers an amazing first-of-its-kind tool for interdisciplinary learning and research. Its focus on works that transformed their disciplines and its rigorous approach, drawing on the world's leading experts and educational institutions, opens up a world-class education to anyone."

—— Andreas Schleicher, Director for Education and Skills, Organisation for Economic Co-operation and Development

"Macat is taking on some of the major challenges in university education... They have drawn together a strong team of active academics who are producing teaching materials that are novel in the breadth of their approach."

—— Prof Lord Broers, former Vice-Chancellor of the University of Cambridge

"The Macat vision is exceptionally exciting. It focuses upon new modes of learning which analyse and explain seminal texts which have profoundly influenced world thinking and so social and economic development. It promotes the kind of critical thinking which is essential for any society and economy. This is the learning of the future."

—— Rt Hon Charles Clarke, former UK Secretary of State for Education

"The Macat analyses provide immediate access to the critical conversation surrounding the books that have shaped their respective discipline, which will make them an invaluable resource to all of those, students and teachers, working in the field."

—— Prof William Tronzo, University of California at San Diego

The Macat Library
世界思想宝库钥匙丛书

TITLE	中文书名	类别
An Analysis of Arjun Appadurai's *Modernity at Large: Cultural Dimensions of Globalization*	解析阿尔君·阿帕杜莱《消失的现代性：全球化的文化维度》	人类学
An Analysis of Claude Lévi-Strauss's *Structural Anthropology*	解析克劳德·列维-斯特劳斯《结构人类学》	人类学
An Analysis of Marcel Mauss's *The Gift*	解析马塞尔·莫斯《礼物》	人类学
An Analysis of Jared M. Diamond's *Guns, Germs, and Steel: The Fate of Human Societies*	解析贾雷德·M.戴蒙德《枪炮、病菌与钢铁：人类社会的命运》	人类学
An Analysis of Clifford Geertz's *The Interpretation of Cultures*	解析克利福德·格尔茨《文化的解释》	人类学
An Analysis of Philippe Ariès's *Centuries of Childhood: A Social History of Family Life*	解析菲力浦·阿利埃斯《儿童的世纪：旧制度下的儿童和家庭生活》	人类学
An Analysis of W. Chan Kim & Renée Mauborgne's *Blue Ocean Strategy*	解析金伟灿/勒妮·莫博涅《蓝海战略》	商业
An Analysis of John P. Kotter's *Leading Change*	解析约翰·P.科特《领导变革》	商业
An Analysis of Michael E. Porter's *Competitive Strategy: Techniques for Analyzing Industries and Competitors*	解析迈克尔·E.波特《竞争战略：分析产业和竞争对手的技术》	商业
An Analysis of Jean Lave & Etienne Wenger's *Situated Learning: Legitimate Peripheral Participation*	解析琼·莱夫/艾蒂纳·温格《情境学习：合法的边缘性参与》	商业
An Analysis of Douglas McGregor's *The Human Side of Enterprise*	解析道格拉斯·麦格雷戈《企业的人性面》	商业
An Analysis of Milton Friedman's *Capitalism and Freedom*	解析米尔顿·弗里德曼《资本主义与自由》	商业
An Analysis of Ludwig von Mises's *The Theory of Money and Credit*	解析路德维希·冯·米塞斯《货币和信用理论》	经济学
An Analysis of Adam Smith's *The Wealth of Nations*	解析亚当·斯密《国富论》	经济学
An Analysis of Thomas Piketty's *Capital in the Twenty-First Century*	解析托马斯·皮凯蒂《21世纪资本论》	经济学
An Analysis of Nassim Nicholas Taleb's *The Black Swan: The Impact of the Highly Improbable*	解析纳西姆·尼古拉斯·塔勒布《黑天鹅：如何应对不可预知的未来》	经济学
An Analysis of Ha-Joon Chang's *Kicking Away the Ladder*	解析张夏准《富国陷阱：发达国家为何踢开梯子》	经济学
An Analysis of Thomas Robert Malthus's *An Essay on the Principle of Population*	解析托马斯·罗伯特·马尔萨斯《人口论》	经济学

An Analysis of John Maynard Keynes's *The General Theory of Employment, Interest and Money*	解析约翰·梅纳德·凯恩斯《就业、利息和货币通论》	经济学
An Analysis of Milton Friedman's *The Role of Monetary Policy*	解析米尔顿·弗里德曼《货币政策的作用》	经济学
An Analysis of Burton G. Malkiel's *A Random Walk Down Wall Street*	解析伯顿·G.马尔基尔《漫步华尔街》	经济学
An Analysis of Friedrich A. Hayek's *The Road to Serfdom*	解析弗里德里希·A.哈耶克《通往奴役之路》	经济学
An Analysis of Charles P. Kindleberger's *Manias, Panics, and Crashes: A History of Financial Crises*	解析查尔斯·P.金德尔伯格《疯狂、惊恐和崩溃：金融危机史》	经济学
An Analysis of Amartya Sen's *Development as Freedom*	解析阿马蒂亚·森《以自由看待发展》	经济学
An Analysis of Rachel Carson's *Silent Spring*	解析蕾切尔·卡森《寂静的春天》	地理学
An Analysis of Charles Darwin's *On the Origin of Species: by Means of Natural Selection, or The Preservation of Favoured Races in the Struggle for Life*	解析查尔斯·达尔文《物种起源》	地理学
An Analysis of World Commission on Environment and Development's *The Brundtland Report: Our Common Future*	解析世界环境与发展委员会《布伦特兰报告：我们共同的未来》	地理学
An Analysis of James E. Lovelock's *Gaia: A New Look at Life on Earth*	解析詹姆斯·E.拉伍洛克《盖娅：地球生命的新视野》	地理学
An Analysis of Paul Kennedy's *The Rise and Fall of the Great Powers: Economic Change and Military Conflict from 1500–2000*	解析保罗·肯尼迪《大国的兴衰：1500—2000年的经济变革与军事冲突》	历史
An Analysis of Janet L. Abu-Lughod's *Before European Hegemony: The World System A. D. 1250–1350*	解析珍妮特·L.阿布－卢格霍德《欧洲霸权之前：1250—1350年的世界体系》	历史
An Analysis of Alfred W. Crosby's *The Columbian Exchange: Biological and Cultural Consequences of 1492*	解析艾尔弗雷德·W.克罗斯比《哥伦布大交换：1492年以后的生物影响和文化冲击》	历史
An Analysis of Tony Judt's *Postwar: A History of Europe since 1945*	解析托尼·朱特《战后欧洲史》	历史
An Analysis of Richard J. Evans's *In Defence of History*	解析理查德·J.艾文斯《捍卫历史》	历史
An Analysis of Eric Hobsbawm's *The Age of Revolution: Europe 1789–1848*	解析艾瑞克·霍布斯鲍姆《革命的年代：欧洲 1789—1848 年》	历史

An Analysis of Roland Barthes's *Mythologies*	解析罗兰·巴特《神话学》	文学与批判理论
An Analysis of Simone de Beauvoir's *The Second Sex*	解析西蒙娜·德·波伏娃《第二性》	文学与批判理论
An Analysis of Edward W. Said's *Orientalism*	解析爱德华·W. 萨义德《东方主义》	文学与批判理论
An Analysis of Virginia Woolf's *A Room of One's Own*	解析弗吉尼亚·伍尔芙《一间自己的房间》	文学与批判理论
An Analysis of Judith Butler's *Gender Trouble*	解析朱迪斯·巴特勒《性别麻烦》	文学与批判理论
An Analysis of Ferdinand de Saussure's *Course in General Linguistics*	解析费尔迪南·德·索绪尔《普通语言学教程》	文学与批判理论
An Analysis of Susan Sontag's *On Photography*	解析苏珊·桑塔格《论摄影》	文学与批判理论
An Analysis of Walter Benjamin's *The Work of Art in the Age of Mechanical Reproduction*	解析瓦尔特·本雅明《机械复制时代的艺术作品》	文学与批判理论
An Analysis of W. E. B. Du Bois's *The Souls of Black Folk*	解析 W.E.B. 杜波依斯《黑人的灵魂》	文学与批判理论
An Analysis of Plato's *The Republic*	解析柏拉图《理想国》	哲学
An Analysis of Plato's *Symposium*	解析柏拉图《会饮篇》	哲学
An Analysis of Aristotle's *Metaphysics*	解析亚里士多德《形而上学》	哲学
An Analysis of Aristotle's *Nicomachean Ethics*	解析亚里士多德《尼各马可伦理学》	哲学
An Analysis of Immanuel Kant's *Critique of Pure Reason*	解析伊曼努尔·康德《纯粹理性批判》	哲学
An Analysis of Ludwig Wittgenstein's *Philosophical Investigations*	解析路德维希·维特根斯坦《哲学研究》	哲学
An Analysis of G. W. F. Hegel's *Phenomenology of Spirit*	解析 G. W. F. 黑格尔《精神现象学》	哲学
An Analysis of Baruch Spinoza's *Ethics*	解析巴鲁赫·斯宾诺莎《伦理学》	哲学
An Analysis of Hannah Arendt's *The Human Condition*	解析汉娜·阿伦特《人的境况》	哲学
An Analysis of G. E. M. Anscombe's *Modern Moral Philosophy*	解析 G. E. M. 安斯康姆《现代道德哲学》	哲学
An Analysis of David Hume's *An Enquiry Concerning Human Understanding*	解析大卫·休谟《人类理解研究》	哲学

An Analysis of Søren Kierkegaard's *Fear and Trembling*	解析索伦·克尔凯郭尔《恐惧与战栗》	哲学
An Analysis of René Descartes's *Meditations on First Philosophy*	解析勒内·笛卡尔《第一哲学沉思录》	哲学
An Analysis of Friedrich Nietzsche's *On the Genealogy of Morality*	解析弗里德里希·尼采《论道德的谱系》	哲学
An Analysis of Gilbert Ryle's *The Concept of Mind*	解析吉尔伯特·赖尔《心的概念》	哲学
An Analysis of Thomas Kuhn's *The Structure of Scientific Revolutions*	解析托马斯·库恩《科学革命的结构》	哲学
An Analysis of John Stuart Mill's *Utilitarianism*	解析约翰·斯图亚特·穆勒《功利主义》	哲学
An Analysis of Aristotle's *Politics*	解析亚里士多德《政治学》	政治学
An Analysis of Niccolò Machiavelli's *The Prince*	解析尼科洛·马基雅维利《君主论》	政治学
An Analysis of Karl Marx's *Capital*	解析卡尔·马克思《资本论》	政治学
An Analysis of Benedict Anderson's *Imagined Communities*	解析本尼迪克特·安德森《想象的共同体》	政治学
An Analysis of Samuel P. Huntington's *The Clash of Civilizations and the Remaking of World Order*	解析塞缪尔·P.亨廷顿《文明的冲突与世界秩序的重建》	政治学
An Analysis of Alexis de Tocqueville's *Democracy in America*	解析阿列克西·德·托克维尔《论美国的民主》	政治学
An Analysis of John A. Hobson's *Imperialism: A Study*	解析约翰·A.霍布森《帝国主义》	政治学
An Analysis of Thomas Paine's *Common Sense*	解析托马斯·潘恩《常识》	政治学
An Analysis of John Rawls's *A Theory of Justice*	解析约翰·罗尔斯《正义论》	政治学
An Analysis of Francis Fukuyama's *The End of History and the Last Man*	解析弗朗西斯·福山《历史的终结与最后的人》	政治学
An Analysis of John Locke's *Two Treatises of Government*	解析约翰·洛克《政府论》	政治学
An Analysis of Sun Tzu's *The Art of War*	解析孙武《孙子兵法》	政治学
An Analysis of Henry Kissinger's *World Order: Reflections on the Character of Nations and the Course of History*	解析亨利·基辛格《世界秩序》	政治学
An Analysis of Jean-Jacques Rousseau's *The Social Contract*	解析让-雅克·卢梭《社会契约论》	政治学

An Analysis of Odd Arne Westad's *The Global Cold War: Third World Interventions and the Making of Our Times*	解析文安立《全球冷战：美苏对第三世界的干涉与当代世界的形成》	政治学
An Analysis of Sigmund Freud's *The Interpretation of Dreams*	解析西格蒙德·弗洛伊德《梦的解析》	心理学
An Analysis of William James' *The Principles of Psychology*	解析威廉·詹姆斯《心理学原理》	心理学
An Analysis of Philip Zimbardo's *The Lucifer Effect*	解析菲利普·津巴多《路西法效应》	心理学
An Analysis of Leon Festinger's *A Theory of Cognitive Dissonance*	解析利昂·费斯汀格《认知失调论》	心理学
An Analysis of Richard H. Thaler & Cass R. Sunstein's *Nudge: Improving Decisions about Health, Wealth, and Happiness*	解析理查德·H. 泰勒 / 卡斯·R. 桑斯坦《助推：如何做出有关健康、财富和幸福的更优决策》	心理学
An Analysis of Gordon Allport's *The Nature of Prejudice*	解析高尔登·奥尔波特《偏见的本质》	心理学
An Analysis of Steven Pinker's *The Better Angels of Our Nature: Why Violence Has Declined*	解析斯蒂芬·平克《人性中的善良天使：暴力为什么会减少》	心理学
An Analysis of Stanley Milgram's *Obedience to Authority*	解析斯坦利·米尔格拉姆《对权威的服从》	心理学
An Analysis of Betty Friedan's *The Feminine Mystique*	解析贝蒂·弗里丹《女性的奥秘》	心理学
An Analysis of David Riesman's *The Lonely Crowd: A Study of the Changing American Character*	解析大卫·理斯曼《孤独的人群：美国人社会性格演变之研究》	社会学
An Analysis of Franz Boas's *Race, Language and Culture*	解析弗朗兹·博厄斯《种族、语言与文化》	社会学
An Analysis of Pierre Bourdieu's *Outline of a Theory of Practice*	解析皮埃尔·布尔迪厄《实践理论大纲》	社会学
An Analysis of Max Weber's *The Protestant Ethic and the Spirit of Capitalism*	解析马克斯·韦伯《新教伦理与资本主义精神》	社会学
An Analysis of Jane Jacobs's *The Death and Life of Great American Cities*	解析简·雅各布斯《美国大城市的死与生》	社会学
An Analysis of C. Wright Mills's *The Sociological Imagination*	解析C. 赖特·米尔斯《社会学的想象力》	社会学
An Analysis of Robert E. Lucas Jr.'s *Why Doesn't Capital Flow from Rich to Poor Countries?*	解析小罗伯特·E. 卢卡斯《为何资本不从富国流向穷国？》	社会学

An Analysis of Émile Durkheim's *On Suicide*	解析埃米尔·迪尔凯姆《自杀论》	社会学
An Analysis of Eric Hoffer's *The True Believer: Thoughts on the Nature of Mass Movements*	解析埃里克·霍弗《狂热分子：群众运动圣经》	社会学
An Analysis of Jared M. Diamond's *Collapse: How Societies Choose to Fail or Survive*	解析贾雷德·M.戴蒙德《大崩溃：社会如何选择兴亡》	社会学
An Analysis of Michel Foucault's *The History of Sexuality Vol. 1: The Will to Knowledge*	解析米歇尔·福柯《性史（第一卷）：求知意志》	社会学
An Analysis of Michel Foucault's *Discipline and Punish*	解析米歇尔·福柯《规训与惩罚》	社会学
An Analysis of Richard Dawkins's *The Selfish Gene*	解析理查德·道金斯《自私的基因》	社会学
An Analysis of Antonio Gramsci's *Prison Notebooks*	解析安东尼奥·葛兰西《狱中札记》	社会学
An Analysis of Augustine's *Confessions*	解析奥古斯丁《忏悔录》	神学
An Analysis of C. S. Lewis's *The Abolition of Man*	解析 C. S. 路易斯《人之废》	神学

图书在版编目（CIP）数据

解析约翰·洛克《政府论》：汉、英 / 杰里米·克莱多斯蒂（Jeremy Kleidosty）
依恩·杰克逊（Ian Jackson）著；曹思宇译. —上海：上海外语教育出版社，202
（世界思想宝库钥匙丛书）
ISBN 978-7-5446-6125-6

Ⅰ.①解… Ⅱ.①杰… ②依… ③曹… Ⅲ.①洛克（Locke, John 1632-1704）—
政治哲学—研究—汉、英 Ⅳ.①B561.24

中国版本图书馆CIP数据核字（2020）第014565号

This Chinese-English bilingual edition of *An Analysis of John Locke's* Two Treatises of
Government is published by arrangement with Macat International Limited.
Licensed for sale throughout the world.

本书汉英双语版由Macat国际有限公司授权上海外语教育出版社有限公司出版。
供在全世界范围内发行、销售。

图字：09 – 2018 – 549

出版发行：上海外语教育出版社
　　　　　　（上海外国语大学内）　邮编：200083
电　　话：021-65425300（总机）
电子邮箱：bookinfo@sflep.com.cn
网　　址：http://www.sflep.com
责任编辑：蒋浚浚

印　　刷：上海叶大印务发展有限公司
开　　本：890×1240　1/32　印张 5.75　字数 118千字
版　　次：2020 年 9 月第 1 版　2020 年 9 月第 1 次印刷
印　　数：2 100 册

书　　号：ISBN 978-7-5446-6125-6
定　　价：30.00 元
　　　　本版图书如有印装质量问题，可向本社调换
　　　　质量服务热线：4008-213-263　电子邮箱：editorial@sflep.com